CHAMPIONSHIP WRITING
50 Ways to Improve Your Writing

by Paula LaRocque

Marion Street Press, Inc.

Cover photo by David Leeson
Cover and interior design by Michelle Crisanti
Copyright © 2000, by Paula LaRocque
All Rights Reserved

Library of Congress Cataloging-in-Publication Data

LaRocque, Paula, 1937-
    Championship writing: 50 ways to improve your writing/by
America's foremost writing coach Paula LaRocque.
    p. cm.
    Includes index.
    ISBN 0-9665176-3-6
1. Journalism—Authorship. I. Title.
    PN4775 .L29 2000
    808'.06607—dc21

                                                  00-011586

ISBN: 0-9665176-3-6

Marion Street Press, Inc.
PO Box 2249
Oak Park, IL 60304
708-445-8330
www.marionstreetpress.com

To the most exacting editors I know:
Paul
Stu
Lennox

About the author

Paula LaRocque, assistant managing editor and writing coach at *The Dallas Morning News*, frequently speaks on effective communication and has conducted writing workshops for scores of newspapers in the United States and Canada. She was a writing consultant for the Associated Press Washington Bureau from 1989 to 1993. She appears regularly on Dallas' NPR station, and she writes a regular column on writing and the language for *Quill* magazine, for *The Dallas Morning News*, and for the *APME News*. A television special, "The Writing Coach, With Paula LaRocque," premiered in Dallas in 1993 and aired periodically on PBS stations across the country.

Paula LaRocque is a writer's writer. And she knows how to probe the writing issues we all face, to define the qualities of lively writing, and to do it all with humor and insight. This book is a must-buy for writers, journalists, and writing teachers. Each chapter models good writing while showing readers practical ways to improve their writing.
—Tommy Thomason, Ed.D., Chairman, *Department of Journalism, Texas Christian University*

Paula LaRocque practices what she preaches. Her writing informs and elevates. It teaches that putting facts together is as important as putting words together. And it brims with examples of good writing from near and far. A good writer, after all, is well-read. These examples of her good advice and good writing prove why her columns in Quill *are well-read, also.*
—Paul McMasters, First Amendment Ombudsman, *The Freedom Forum*

table of
contents

Introduction

This work is based on one chief assumption: That good writing is clear, precise, graceful, brief and warm, and that bad writing is not. It also supposes that if informational writing is to work, it must be both understandable and understood.

The columns in this collection appeared originally in *Quill*, the Society of Professional Journalists' magazine. They were written largely for media writers, whether in print, television, radio or the Web, or in advertising or public relations. The work pertains to all workplace writing, however, because all workplace writing is (or should be) informational.

Why does workplace writing so often fail to do what it's supposed to do — that is, convey information accurately, simply, clearly, briefly? I believe the answer is twofold: education and lack of education. Unfortunately, education can hinder clear and brief communication because academe often rewards another kind of writing — stiff, dense, pretentious, glutted with gobbledygook and arcane phrasing. We've all seen examples of academic gibberish — no need to document that here. It's enough to note that the educated often bring academe's heavy and unconversational writing style into the workplace, and that it is unwelcome. Writing can be like unrefined or refined jewels: Raw stones are murky and rough; polished gems are clear and smooth. With words, the hard work of editing provides the refinement, as Mark Twain obliquely observed when he wrote: "I would have written you a shorter letter, but I didn't have the time."

Lack of education also can hinder good communication because the poorly educated may not have mastered Standard English — and Standard English is critical to good writing. Errors in grammar, structure and usage lose not only precision but also the reader's respect. It's a matter of trust — we don't trust "experts" who can't use their tools, and the language is the only tool the writer has. Some of the columns in this book deal with common errors, but you can find a wealth of material on English mechanics in libraries and bookstores. It's worth the effort: Your work will gain in authority and believability.

My publisher asked me if I wanted to include acknowledgments. I said no. Most of us are sums of the effort spent on us, and once we begin thanking people, there's no end to it. I do, however, want to acknowledge one special person's influence and support for more than 25 years — that of my husband, Paul LaRocque.

Arlington, Texas
August 2000

1

Short and simple

Fuzzy writers force readers to do their work

Clarity is crucial to good writing of any kind. Whether the
communication is a news story, press release, letter, memo or
report, its merit rests on its understandability. If it's unclear, it
can only bewilder, annoy or mislead.

The two basic qualities of clear writing are comfortingly
simple. The first is brevity, and the second is simplicity. Length
is critical — whether of word, sentence, paragraph or finished
piece. And while a simple and accessible subject might seem
necessary to clear communication, it isn't. That's the whole point:
Making the content simple and accessible is the writer's job.
Clear writing is the product of thoughtful communicators who
not only understand the subject, but know how to make others
understand it, too.

For example, watch the story emerge in this newspaper writer's
work. He rewrote his dense and uninviting lead after a workshop
on clear writing. See how the story — the only thing that inter-
ests readers — is lost in the original but found in the clear and
attractive revision.

Original: *A major reassessment that could lead to big changes in Orange County's public transportation system is beginning, prompted in part by a new anti-smog law that is boosting business' demand for better service.*

Revision: *Local government leaders want to make it easier for Orange County residents to get around without their cars.*

The difference between those two passages is the difference between unclear and clear writing. The rewritten version goes beyond a literal transcription of the original and is the product of fresh thinking about how to tell a story. To rewrite, the author asked himself:

- what was most interesting about the story.
- how it might affect people.
- how he would tell it if he were telling it.

Those questions helped him to write a clear, interesting story rather than a fuzzy, dull *report*.

Although the argument for clarity is too obvious and sound to reject, some writers still resist. They come close to suggesting that the work can't or even shouldn't be perfectly clear. Of course, they can't sensibly say they prefer muddy, pretentious, careless prose. So they say something more acceptable — that it isn't really weak or that it's weak for good reasons.

Or they criticize the clear version: *That's an over-simplification.* Or: *Well, that dumbs it down a bit.* Or: *This muddy writing that the average intelligent person can't understand is actually clearer and more precise, if you know the specialized language.*

All that is sophistry. Good, clear writing is neither dumb nor oversimple (unless it's also written by the unintelligent). And unclear writing is self-indulgent if not arrogant.

The truth is that the best communicators are and have always been the clearest communicators — from Winston Churchill to Albert Einstein. They've learned that knowledge isn't worth much if we can't convey it to others. The same principle applies to creative writing as well. Authors who create work known for its purity and excellence also create work known for its simplicity. Ernest Hemingway and F. Scott Fitzgerald spring to mind. So do contemporary writers such as John McPhee or Joan Didion. Norman Maclean's *A River Runs Through It* is admired for its restraint, clarity and plain language. Exceptions such as James Joyce or William Faulkner are known for innovation rather than clarity. But those authors were trying to create new forms and, face it, most readers of works such as *Finnegans Wake* are reading it for a seminar — in other words, because they *have* to.

Even knowing all that, many writers still resist applying the principles of clarity to their work. They don't want to change. And they don't want to do the careful, thoughtful work that clear writing demands — they want the *readers* to do it. Here, from a press release, is the kind of writing that results:

To enhance the federal government's ability to address emerging issues and minimize conflict among goals for environmental quality, energy security, and economic strength, a task force of the Commission on Science, Technology, and Government has urged creation of a strong top-level institutional mechanism in the Executive Branch to provide policy analyses and policy direction to the president.

That writing is incomprehensible. Aside from the problems of length, density and arcane vocabulary, what is a "top-level institutional mechanism"? Is it a person, a committee, another agency? We don't know, and there's no way to tell without consulting the writer. To rewrite, let's assume that a "top-level institutional

13

mechanism" is a committee.

A government task force has asked the president to form an environmental committee to advise him on environmental issues. The committee, recommended by the Commission on Science, Technology, and Government, would also would seek to reduce conflict with other special interest groups.

This rewritten version shows that shorter, more conversational sentences promote clarity. It also suggests that when dealing with complex material, it's usually better to begin with a general, clear statement and add specifics in later paragraphs.

On the purpose of ink

Octopus writing sinks readers in a sea of words

How much of the following writing do you understand?

I devise and bequeath all the residue of my property whatsoever and wheresoever to which I shall be entitled or of which I shall have power to dispose at my death to the Trustees upon trust to sell call in and convert into money such part thereof as shall not already consist of money with power to postpone such sale calling in and conversion so long as the Trustees shall in their absolute discretion think fit and so that no reversionary interest shall be sold until it falls into possession unless the Trustees see special reason for sale and so that the provisions of clause 13 hereof shall apply in regard to the administration of my estate.

Any sentence of such length written mostly in prepositional phrases would spell chaos, yet this lawyer still forces it on his client. Or how about the following course description, which an English professor visited upon his students:

This course is a study of recent social, historical, intellectual, and geographical change through examination of social, literary, electronic discourses and through exploration of private and public change. It includes the study of how, when, why, or whether marked personal and public dislocations are accompanied by manifestations of nostalgia, fail-

ures or rearrangements of private and public memory, and conflicts among competing rhetorics, with attendant apprehensiveness regarding loss of personal and public value and identity. The course proposes specific cases for study and the development of useful and generative patterns of critical analysis.

I think of such prose as "octopus writing" because, to an octopus, the function of ink is not to reveal but to obscure. We don't have to be lawyers, academics, technicians or bureaucrats to assault readers with verbal fog. All we have to do is forget the most basic principles of good writing — in fact, of any good communication — and instead:

- Write as long as possible before using a period.
- Use arcane, abstract or unnecessary words.
- Publish rough drafts rather than finished work.

Fine and memorable writing is fine and memorable because of its simplicity — because the writer has taken the time to rewrite and refine. Abraham Lincoln's speech at Gettysburg is renowned not for highfalutin rhetoric, but for the natural stateliness and clarity of simplicity. Winston Churchill also insisted on simplicity, and his words moved millions:

We shall fight on the beaches, we shall fight on the landing grounds, we shall fight in the fields and in the streets, we shall fight in the hills.

What if, instead of that passage, Churchill had offered an inky cloud — as in the following version by Richard Mitchell in *Less Than Words Can Say*? Would millions have assembled to hear and be moved by his words?

Consolidated defensive positions and essential pre-planned withdrawal facilities are to be provided in order to facilitate maximum potentialization for the repulsion and/or delay of incursive combatants in each of several pre-identified categories of location deemed suitable to the emplacement and/or debarkation of hostile military contingents.

On the purpose of ink

Octopus writing means losing control of the proper craft of writing — the craft that lays meaning bare, that reveals rather than conceals. Here's a passage from a movie critic who loses control of his craft:

Forced in anguish to abandon his real family for his Mob family — his wife, whose patience with his absences finally runs out, is very well played by Anne Heche — Brasco must ultimately betray his only real friend in the criminal clan, Al Pacino's very weary, very unsuccessful and finally very touching soldier, a man the movie makes much more appealing than the law-enforcement bureaucrats who show not an ounce of understanding, let alone compassion, for the soul Pistone-Brasco has shriven in their service.

How might this passage read if the reviewer practiced good craft? First, he would use some periods. Second, he would stick to one main idea per sentence. Third, he'd skip vague qualifiers such as *very* and arcane words such as *shriven*. Then he might write:

Brasco's wife, well played by Anne Heche, finally loses patience with his absences. An anguished Brasco is forced to abandon his real family for his Mob family and ultimately must betray his only real friend in the criminal clan, played by Al Pacino. The movie makes Pacino's weary, unsuccessful, and finally touching soldier more appealing than the police bureaucrats who show not an ounce of understanding, let alone compassion, for the soul Brasco has sacrificed in their service.

Fuzzy writing always reflects fuzzy thought. Lack of conversational grace and simplicity is bad because it fails to please. But lack of clarity is worse because it fails to inform.

People will little note nor long remember a cluttered sentence

Lincoln's restraint made words at Gettysburg timeless

One of the media writer's most critical tasks — yet a relatively easy one — is cutting clutter. Clutter compromises all artistry — and in writing, clutter means prepositions, particles, lazy or repetitive words. Even excellent writers can forget the hazards of deadwood and be seduced by length and weight — to the detriment of clarity.

Oddly, perfect clarity can be unnerving — even to journalists, who profess to deal in it. Perfect clarity is so assertive, so unequivocal, so. . . *clear*. We're often more comfortable when we've blurred things a bit with words that drain off energy but add no content. So we write:

Spurred by a need to salve economic wounds at home, Japanese investors have sharply accelerated their retreat from the U.S. real estate market they galloped into last decade, said a study released Thursday.

That lead, which combines clutter with clumsy structure and runaway metaphor, shows how important restraint is to good writing:

Japanese investors are leaving the U.S. real estate market in the

'90s almost as fast as they entered it in the '80s, says a study released Thursday. Economic distress at home is one of the factors. . . .

Clutter is its worst when it's cumulative. One sentence with a few too many words becomes several sentences with far too many words — until the whole piece could be reduced by a third without losing a single significant idea or image. A newspaper story reads: "In 1919, a young soldier named Dwight D. Eisenhower first thought up the idea of an interstate highway system." That's a good sentence, but it could be a *fine* sentence if it traded "first thought up the idea of" for one active verb: "In 1919, a young soldier named Dwight D. Eisenhower *imagined* an interstate highway system."

Active verbs not only cut clutter, they also strengthen and clarify meaning. Flabby writing often turns active verbs into "ing" verbs plus auxiliaries: *He was wearing; she was sitting; they were meeting* — rather than *he wore; she sat; they met.* "Residents expect the sports center to keep growing," writes a reporter, when a better rendition would be "Residents expect the sports center to grow." Another example:

Motorists have been smiling and gasoline dealers have been gritting their teeth over a local gasoline price war that has pushed some of the lowest gasoline prices in more than a decade even lower.

That bungled lead also suffers a repetitive headline: "Local gas war brings smiles at pump," which steals from the writer only to add more flab. Trimmer and more purposeful:

Gasoline prices are at their lowest in more than a decade, but a local price war is pushing them even lower — to motorist's delight and dealer's dismay.

Prepositions and clutter are close friends:

For John Damon, his friend and travel partner Diane Ferris, and their families, the story hit close to home as the pair returned just a

*month ago from a holiday that took them to the very spot where vaca-
tioners from the United states, the United Kingdom, New Zealand,
Australia and Switzerland were grabbed by the terrorists.*

Cutting clutter reveals the sentence's intent: "The story
alarmed John Damon and Diane Ferris because they recently visited the spot where the terrorists abducted the tourists."

Even one unnecessary preposition can damage a sentence's
flow. This one has five — about two too many: "Dangling a cigarette out the window of his cruiser, the trooper squints at the
traffic roaring eastbound on Interstate 70 through a light rain."

Prepositions aside, a cigarette in rain — even a light rain — is
an unnecessary distraction. Good description doesn't slavishly
record random details or details that fight with each other. If the
weather mattered, it could be added later. But it doesn't matter —
this story is about drug traffic on I-70; the focus is traffic and
highway. That's about as much as one sentence can handle anyway: "The trooper dangles a cigarette out the cruiser window and
squints at the I-70 traffic roaring eastward." Or, if we wanted the
weather: "A light rain falls on I-70, and the trooper peers through
his cruiser window at the traffic roaring eastward."

Good writing means making choices.

Redundancies are obvious contributors to wordiness: *past history, past experience, end result, sum total, basic fundamentals, free
gift, true fact, repeat again, set a new record, personal friendship, 12
noon, 12 midnight, close down, strangled to death, root cause, total
effect, large in size, potential promise.*

Quotations also can clutter. Speech is notoriously wordy, but
the paraphrase can help. Consider: "He said he has many times
expressed his desire to step down from his position as director of
the transportation department." The source probably said exactly
that, but then why paraphrase? The point of the paraphrase is to

trim quotes to their essence: "He said he has asked repeatedly to leave his post as transportation director."

Clear, simple, brief communication is the most meaningful and memorable communication. We should trust it more. Abraham Lincoln spoke only two minutes at Gettysburg; the main orator of the day, Edward Everett, spoke nearly two hours. Yet who remembers Edward Everett, or what he said?

Wordiness

Never so bethump'd with words!

The writer's worst enemies are deadwood and redundancies. The two are not the same things: Although all redundancy is wordy, all wordiness is not redundant. Simply, deadwood means words that do no work, and redundancy means words that do the same work.

Until we've edited for deadwood and redundancy, we still have the roughest of drafts, one in which the message is obscured rather than revealed. Once the unnecessary words are cut, however, we have a firm foundation upon which to build greater meaning and clarity.

One path to wordiness lies in pairing "-ion" nouns (*investigation, exhibition, decision*) with verbs such as *get, take, make,* or *give*. In such structures, both noun and verb are weakened by the presence of the other. It's better if the verb form of the "-ion" word stands alone. Thus, "conduct an investigation into" becomes "investigate"; "give an exhibition" becomes "exhibit"; "make a decision" becomes "decide."

Another sign of deadwood is seen in the preposition — notice that prepositions often appear in the wordy expressions below. Pruning prepositions is usually one way to leaner writing. Thus, "he took a position in close proximity to the entrance of the apartment building" becomes "he positioned himself near the apartment building entrance."

It's good to write conversationally, but the more conversational the work, the greater the certainty that it will be wordy. That's because speech is wordy — we haven't the luxury of editing. If we write conversationally *and* edit for precision, however, we'll have the best of both skills. Spare, precise, active writing is not only shorter and clearer, it is also more interesting and energetic.

conduct an investigation into: INVESTIGATE

during the course of the investigation: DURING THE INVESTIGATION

made the statement that: SAID

at a later date: LATER

were found to be in agreement: AGREED

succeed in making: MAKE

make use of, utilize: USE

procure: GET, BUY

were in attendance: ATTENDED

crisis situation: CRISIS

despite the fact that: ALTHOUGH

prior to: BEFORE

subsequent to: AFTER

reside: LIVE

indicate: SHOW, SAY, SUGGEST

say they are of the opinion: SAY THEY THINK, BELIEVE

on the occasion that: WHEN

give consideration to: CONSIDER

have the need for: NEED

made an effort: TRIED

in conjunction with: WITH

as to whether: WHETHER

until such time as: UNTIL

with the exception of: EXCEPT

in all other cases: OTHERWISE

a sufficient number of: ENOUGH

in the vicinity of: NEAR

located at: AT

on a daily basis: DAILY

on a regular basis: REGULARLY

on an experimental basis: EXPERIMENTALLY

by the same token: LIKEWISE, SIMILARLY

which is called: CALLED

continue on: CONTINUE

a distance of 35 miles: 35 MILES

of an irreversible nature: IRREVERSIBLE

has the ability to: CAN

said he was not in a position to: SAID HE COULDN'T

escalated to a dangerous level: ROSE DANGEROUSLY

said in a quiet tone of voice: SAID QUIETLY

the reason is because: THE REASON IS

the reason why he: THE REASON HE

nodded her head: NODDED

shrugged his shoulders: SHRUGGED

a number of; a small number of; few in number:
    SOME, SEVERAL, FEW

Wordiness

in this day and age; at this point; at present; at this point in time: NOW

it would seem that; it would appear that: APPARENTLY, EVIDENTLY

in the nature of; along the lines of: LIKE

in view of the fact that; on account of the fact that; for the reason that: BECAUSE, SINCE

pertaining to; in connection with; in reference to; with/in regard to: ABOUT

in the amount of; for the purpose of: FOR

to be in a position to; in order to; with a view toward: TO

in the event that; if it should turn out that: IF

past history; past experience: HISTORY, EXPERIENCE

end result: RESULT

sum total: TOTAL

root cause: CAUSE

total effect: EFFECT

basic fundamentals: FUNDAMENTALS (or BASICS)

consensus of opinion: CONSENSUS

potential promise: POTENTIAL (or PROMISE)

free gift; free pass: GIFT, PASS

true fact: FACT

repeat again, reiterate: REPEAT

referred back to: REFERRED TO

dates back to: DATES TO

set a new record: SET A RECORD

large in size: LARGE

round in shape: ROUND

rested up, divided up, finished up, up until: RESTED,
    DIVIDED, FINISHED, UNTIL
personal friendship: FRIENDSHIP
strangled to death: STRANGLED
at about 10 p.m.: AT 10 p.m. or ABOUT 10 p.m.
12 noon; 12 midnight: NOON, MIDNIGHT
close down: CLOSE
close up: CLOSE
equally as good: EQUALLY GOOD

column

5

The writing path can be bumpy or smooth

The building blocks of sentences pave the way

Good writing is the cumulative effect of well-chosen words, but we sometimes don't pay proper attention to those smallest and most basic units of communication. Finding the right words often makes the difference between mediocre and distinguished work. The right words are also critical in writing interesting stories rather than boring reports.

Concrete expression is one of the most important considerations in word choice. Concrete terms are solid and specific, while abstractions blur meaning. Unfortunately, abstraction is often a given in media writing. We can do little, for example, about the long, pretentious and often meaningless proper nouns that title bureaucracies, departments, documents, positions, events, and so forth. It helps to offer readers a clear, brief and generic label in the lead, but sooner or later — if it's the subject of the story — we'll have to identify that subject by its burdensome but official name.

If the necessary abstraction is unfortunate, the *unnecessary* abstraction is abominable. Why choose abstractions when concrete words abound? Why write "indicate," for example, when we could write *show, say,* or *suggest?* "Thunderstorm activity" should be *thun-*

derstorm. "Surgical intervention" should be *surgery.*

The more concrete the term, the more it shows: *a small white dog in a colorful vest* could be, instead, the more evocative *white Chihuahua in a red plaid vest.*

Short and familiar words also promote concrete expression. Short words are small, strong and suited to story-telling: *love, hate, life, death, friend, foe, food, drink, blood, free, save.* Long words are bulky, weak and suited to reports. Short words reveal characters and conflict — two necessary ingredients of story-telling — while long and abstract words *conceal* characters and conflict. Consider this newspaper lead:

A dozen Hamilton residents accused in a civil suit of an alleged loan fraud against the Federal Department of Housing and Urban Development might settle the case before it goes to trial, according to federal court documents.

That passage reads like a report, but watch the *story* emerge when the language is concrete:

A dozen Hamilton residents charged with lying to get U.S. home loans might settle the case before trial.

That's a better beginning — it's clear and conversational and gives us something to build on. We can discuss the Federal Department of Housing and Urban Development and federal court documents later — *after* we've won the reader's interest.

Try to get interested in the lead below:

United Nations officials on Tuesday said that they had intelligence information indicating that Iraq had attempted to mislead United Nation investigators by misrepresenting and understating its nuclear weapons program and the amount of weapons-grade nuclear material it now possesses.

The writer of that lead defended it by saying it was "sensitive diplomatic language." Nonsense. It's nothing more than poor writing, a simple message made complicated by flim flam. How would it read in short, simple and concrete words? Maybe: *The United Nations said Tuesday that Iraq had purposely understated its nuclear weapon stores.*

Short and concrete words help avoid bombast. They could have rescued the writer of the passage below:

The state air control board is initiating a Strategic Enforcement Priorities Plan, a plan which will create a more multi-faceted, more effective enforcement program characterized by placing a heavier emphasis on strategic priorities and targeting use of resources.

Concreteness, with its affinity for short and familiar words, is also more conversational. It lends warmth and humanity. If we faithfully write much as we speak, we will write stories rather than reports. A good guideline: If we couldn't or wouldn't say it that way, we probably shouldn't write it that way, either. The unsayable is also the unreadable.

It goes without saying that those who speak poorly probably will write poorly as well — whatever their style. But that consideration aside, there are two hazards in writing as we speak: deadwood and vague qualifiers. Speech is notoriously wordy. So the task is to write conversationally, then to edit mercilessly to remove the padding.

Speech also contains many vague qualifiers. Avoid them in writing, generally — find the precise word, one that won't have to be qualified. Words such as *really, very, truly, extremely, basically, totally, quite, rather, somewhat,* etc., are valuable in speech because they allow us to use the less-than-precise word. We can't keep listeners waiting while we search for exactly the right word, so we buttress weak words with modifiers such as *very* or *extremely*, and we reduce words that are too strong with modifiers such as *rather* or *somewhat*. In writing, however, we can be more reflective and selective. Fewer qualifiers means tighter, clearer, more concrete work.

"Very angry" (or, worse, "very, very angry") becomes *furious*.

Words can be likened to the bricks that make up a walkway. Whether the way is smooth and easy depends upon the fit of each brick. Or, as Mark Twain more aptly put it: "The difference between the right word and the nearly right word is the same as the difference between lightning and the lightning bug."

6

Short words

Simple phrasing protects clarity

Making difficult or challenging content easy to grasp depends in part upon how well writers themselves think. Writing clearly means thinking clearly — it involves keen analysis, logic, creativity and precision as well as intellect. As George Orwell observed, fuzzy writing *always* reveals fuzzy thinking.

But say thinking is not a problem. Then all we must do is focus on form. How shall we deliver the result of our careful thought? Which device or style will make our work clear, accurate, brief and compelling? If the form is dense and larded with difficult language, all our painstaking thought will be wasted.

For clarity, we need an open, informal, conversational style. Our schooling has taught us — wrongly, I think — to make a distinction between formal and informal communication, and that formal is superior to informal. The result is a professional world that spouts stiff, pompous, abstract and often meaningless jargon.

An effective but easy way to make difficult work clear is to use one-syllable words as much as possible. The result is neither oversimple nor without sophistication — conversely, wrapping the message in simple language yields both precision and warmth.

Proper nouns and words that can't be shortened without losing meaning are exempt from this effort, but simplifying even *some* of the language will make the message clearer and more compelling.

Here is the top of a wire story, followed by a short-word version. Original:

Energy Secretary Bill Richardson on Monday promised continued economic support for wind energy research and development and support for tax incentives in announcing a plan to increase the country's capacity to get power from wind.

Richardson committed the government to have wind power produce 5 percent of the nation's electrical needs by 2020. Currently, about one-tenth of one percent of the nation's electric needs are provided by the wind.

'We want tomorrow's generators to produce power at half the cost of today's machines,' Richardson said at a wind energy conference. 'That is no small challenge, but this government is committed to making that goal a reality.'

In 1980 wind energy cost about 40 cents per kilowatt hour. Now it's about a nickel.

In addition to the so-called Wind Powering America initiative, Richardson announced $1.2 million in grants to wind turbine testing projects in 10 states. One of those projects will be in Maine. He did not say where the other nine would be.

The money will be used to provide support for the design and installation of new small wind turbines for field testing.

Richardson's message was welcome news to wind power advocates from across the country.

The original has 197 words. Here is a short-word version by Clay Morton of *The Dallas Morning News*. It has 128 words, but it's not just shorter. It's clearer and more interesting — as well as more polished and graceful.

The drive to turn wind into watts got a boost Monday from U.S. Energy Secretary Bill Richardson, who pledged more cash and tax breaks for the cause.

He vowed that wind would fill 5 percent of U.S. electrical needs by 2020, up from 0.1 percent now. It was a promise that pleased those who want wind to help take the place of fuels such as coal and gas.

'We want tomorrow's generators to produce power at half the cost of today's machines,' he said.

In 1980 wind energy cost 40 cents per kilowatt hour. Now it's five cents.

One more thing: Richardson said $1.2 million in grants would pay to test wind turbines. The test states will include Maine, as well as nine others Richardson did not name.

Below, an Idaho reporter turns two of his leads into short-word versions. Which do you like better?

Original: "Thirty-one Magic Valley residents accused in a civil suit of an alleged loan fraud against the Federal Department of Housing and Urban Development might settle the case before it goes to trial, according to federal court documents."

Short-word version: "Thirty-one Magic Valley residents might cut a deal on the charge that they lied to get U.S.-backed home loans."

Original: "As they did in the summer of 1989, proponents of a Community Block Development Grant to improve Highway 93 in front of the Crossroads of Idaho truck stop near Interstate 84 ran into a hornets' nest of opposition at a public hearing Wednesday night."

Short-word version: "Those who want a state grant to fix the road in front of a truck stop on Highway 93 found few who liked the plan Wednesday night."

The original versions are report-writing leads, while the short-word versions are story-telling leads. The story's characters and conflict are obscured by abstraction in the originals, but revealed in the more concrete short-word versions. The revisions leave "Federal Department of Housing and Urban Development" and "Community Block Development Grant" for later in the story, thus freeing the writer to focus on what the stories are *about*.

Memorable language is usually simplified language. It emulates speech at its best and is immediate in its clarity and beauty. If it's also "informal," so much the better.

7

In a surprise move. . . .

Do journalists speak as they write?
If they did, here's how it would sound.

Hack: How were things at your vacation facility?

Frack: We had wide-ranging weather all season. One storm dumped more than seven inches of rain on our densely wooded lot, spawning hurricane-force winds and golfball-sized hail. Plus an unprecedented number of visitors arrived amid the facility restoration.

H: My, that must have sparked burgeoning confusion and decimated your plans for restoring your vacation site to a state-of-the-art facility. Was it sort of a defining moment?

F: It spurred a major shift in sleeping arrangements, triggered sweeping changes in the menu, and fueled a personal economic crunch.

H: What a chilling effect! How long were you beleaguered by this worst-case scenario?

F: The visitors left early, actually, but not before offending everyone, including a close friend and lifelong politician who hails from New

Surprise move

York City and has close ethnic ties.

H: You say your friend is from delegate-rich New York?

F: Right. Anyway, yet another politician friend, D-Dallas, weighed in on the issue by calling for the visitors' immediate withdrawal from my vacation site. And that provoked a firestorm of criticism.

H: Awesome. Did that level the playing field and cause the visitors to leave your strife-torn facility?

F: Heck no. That was just the cutting edge. Next, they targeted my housekeeper, 45, and launched an unprovoked attack.

H: You mean they fired a broadside at her, too? Did a heated debate ensue? Did they hurl verbal insults at each other?

F: Too true. In effect, they unleashed a new round of difficulty, and the whole matter escalated to what some called "critical mass."

H: Which side blinked finally?

F: Well, in a bizarre twist, our embattled housekeeper resigned amid allegations of wrongdoing.

H: Too bad! Your guests actually cited instances of infractions?

F: Oh, a litany. Even a laundry list. But we're in the midst of negotiations and may be able to reinstate the popular employee.

H: Is the bottom line that there's a thin line between a soft and a hard line?

Surprise move

F: So it seems. In the wake of the controversy, there was a sharp decrease in the number of visitors to the summer facility.

H: A sudden downturn, a free fall, or a steep decline, I guess. Should we call it a sea change or a ground swell? Anyway, looks like you've won a stunning victory. Better than a staggering defeat any day!

F: I'm cautiously optimistic. But the same scenario could repeat itself all over again next year.

H: Déja vu!

Fadspeak

Gag me to the max fer sure

Clichés can be divided into three categories. One is the cliché that, poor thing that it is, will always be with us: *sharp as a tack, brown as a berry, slept like a log.* These are both common and innocuous in speech, but less so in writing. They're so trite and flat, in fact, that we'd seldom find them in any writing of serious intent.

Clichés in the second category have more currency, but are easily recognized as clichés. That very recognizability makes them valuable in writing — *if* we change them so they're something *besides* predictable. A writer discussing lawyer advertising, for example, wrote that the issue had opened "Pandora's briefcase." Another, writing of the increasing number of women bikers, said those women wanted a "vroom of their own."

Journalese constitutes a cliché-*like* style of writing: *firestorm of criticism, unprecedented, cautious optimism.* But the words and phrases in that collection of hackery are not properly identified as clichés. They're just part of a trite and easy lexicon.

The third and worst category of cliché is faddish expression. Fadspeak is mimickry, the province of the entirely unoriginal, and is often (happily) short-lived. Much fadspeak derives from television.

Fadspeak

And, like most fads, the robotic responses of Laugh-Track Land become unbearable after a while. We seldom hear *Would you believe?* or *Sorry about that* these days. Seldom heard as well is *Isn't that special?* The sit-com had a mercifully brief fling with Valley Girl lingo such as *gag me with a spoon, to the max,* and *fer sure.* But *Been there, done that* and *Yesss!* are still (tiresomely) with us.

We could do a dissertation, doubtless, on *why* we'd rather ape the fake dialogue of fake characters living fake lives than make real-life conversation. For one thing, such knee-jerkery requires no thought. But because anything that substitutes for original thought and expression *must* promote the hackneyed, dependence upon the latest language fad is particularly dangerous for writers and editors. Consider the finest wordsmiths you know: They use pop-phrases only seldom, often guiltily, and usually kiddingly. (An excellent writer at *The Dallas Morning News* recently responded to another writer's "Get a life!" with "Get a vocabulary!")

Here's the kind of canned clutter media writers would do well to avoid unless they're trying for special effects:

Been there, done that.

Get real.

Get a life.

Get over it.

Go for it.

Suck it up.

Deal with it.

Handle it.

Whatever.

Excuuuuse me.

The mother of all. . . .

Yesss!

Fadspeak

Your worst nightmare.

Just do it.

Duh.

Yeah, right.

Don't go there.

I don't *think* so.

In your dreams.

Hel-*lo*-oh!

I hate when that happens.

The . . . from Hell.

Are we having fun yet?

Time flies when you're. . . .

Yadda, yadda, yadda.

Not even close.

Oh, puh-leeze.

Git outta town!

No-brainer.

[He's, she's, you're] history.

Clueless.

You don't have to be a rocket scientist.

You don't have to be a brain surgeon.

What's wrong with this picture?

What's up wi' dat?

I'm down with that.

Doesn't get it.

Same old same old.

In your face.

It's *so* over.

I'm outta here.

9

Overwriting

Literature's Elvis on velvet

Overwriting immediately damages and lengthens prose of any kind. The relationship between awful writing and overwriting is so well-known that the Lord Bulwer-Lytton bad writing contest chooses for its winner the year's best (read *worst*) overwriting.

Overwriting is the failure to make choices. It's tasteless in the way a lack of control is always tasteless, finally. That's because good taste — in art as in life — invariably involves restraint. Linguistic bric-a-brac is literature's Elvis on velvet.

Most writers overwrite, especially in a work's early stages. But that first editing should blow off the chaff. Until sound self-editing cuts the obvious, the repetitious, the gratuitous, the ugly, the contradictory and the unnecessary, the work is still a rough draft.

Consider this lead from a newspaper profile of author James Lee Burke.

1) *The Bayou Teche is pockmarked with bubbling, moss-green lumps that very well might be knotty-headed gators submarining and cracking the surface of the caramel-colored water. Long beards of Spanish moss are flapping from the cypress and oak trees, convulsing like*

ominous old men guarding a graveyard.

2) James Lee Burke is walking along the familiar, humid paths lining the bayou, deep in the smothering confines of southern Louisiana, not far from the small city where almost every narrow alley and turn-of-the century building groan with some bit of history left behind by long-gone members of his family.

3) Almost every day he is able, Mr. Burke, 61, is here absorbing and revisiting the soul of the place — and the unseen souls who still trudge through here.

This writer's unwillingness or inability to make choices damages a promising beginning. Let's look at the details:

Paragraph 1: "Pockmarked" cannot apply to "lumps" — a pock or pockmark is a pit, a hole, a dent, a depression. "Bubbling moss-green lumps" is inaccurate because it's the water that is bubbling, not the lumps. The first sentence has too many hyphenated structures: "moss-green," "knotty-headed," "caramel-colored." *Moss* is repeated inadvertently and without purpose: "moss-green," "Spanish moss." "Bubbling" and "caramel-colored" are pretty images that detract from the passage's ominous imagery. The phrasing is excessive and contradictory in "gators submarining and cracking the surface." And "convulsing like ominous old men guarding a graveyard" is as ridiculous as it is unnecessary.

Last, is a simple description of place enough to open this profile? Scene-setting beginnings are easy, often overdone and sometimes inappropriate to the piece. They can work, however, if they have a dual purpose: to help say something important about the subject, and to offer a way into the story.

Paragraph 2 has too many prepositions for readability, and its phrasing is flabby overall. "Is walking along" equals *walks*. "Deep in the smothering confines" and "history left behind" are redundant.

"Turn-of-the century building": *Victorian* is more precise and evocative. The alleys and buildings "groan with some bit of history": It's absurd to use "groan" with a "bit"; *groan* suggests considerable weight.

Paragraph 3: The formulaic journalese of "Burke, 61" should be scrapped. This is a story, not a report. The age should be incorporated and made pertinent. Finally, the phrasing "absorbing and revisiting the soul of the place – and the unseen souls who still trudge through here" is classic, mawkish overwriting and should be cut.

Here's the same passage, edited for precision, focus, purpose, compression and beauty:

"The Bayou Teche is James Lee Burke's most frequent haunt. Along its familiar paths, deep in the swamps of southern Louisiana, green bulges that could be knotty-headed gators occasionally break the bayou's tawny surface. Long beards of Spanish moss sway ominously from cypress and oak. And not far lies New Iberia, whose narrow alleys and Victorian buildings recall Burke's long-gone forebears.

"At 61, the writer still finds in this place not only the soul of his family, but also the soul of his art."

Media writers and editors sometimes mistake the blather and bombast of overwriting for "literary" writing. But there's nothing literary about it. Bad prose is as unwelcome in novels as it is in newspapers.

Make stories speak to readers

If your copy doesn't talk the talk, your audience might not hear

Newswriting, whether hard or soft, too often reads like a bureaucratic report rather than a story. It seldom resembles the tale we might tell our friends. Instead, our efforts to add color and verve often create overwrought, self-conscious, or pretentious work.

In short, we tend to make communication more difficult and less natural than it is. Even journalists whose speech is clear, direct and punchy can be strained and artificial on paper.

Why is that? For one thing, we try too hard. We forget that our main concern is imparting information and focus instead on impressing. Imagery, metaphor and description are a writer's stock-in-trade, but without restraint, message can be lost in device.

Droning dullness and overwriting can stem from the same problem — forgetting that good writing is little more than good speech on paper. The simplistic admonition "write as you speak" is hardly the answer, however. Saner counsel would be to "write as you speak if you speak *well*." And a useful companion principle would be not to write what you could not or would not say.

The following lead appeared above the fold on the front page of a leading national newspaper:

Make stories speak

Five hundred years of European colonialism in Asia sputters to a close here this weekend on a desolate, rain-swept waterfront dredged out of Macao's once beguiling harbor. At the stroke of midnight on Sunday, China will reclaim this tiny enclave from Portugal, raising its red flag over another patch of Chinese soil and setting the stage for what it hopes will be eventual reunification with Taiwan.

Aside from the glut of image and preposition, is this effective story-telling and message-bearing? The answers to a few vital questions tell us that it is not:

- Can you imagine saying this to anyone?
- What does this overwrought description finally *mean*? Exactly what is a "tiny enclave" — in terms we can immediately understand?
- Granting that the waterfront may indeed be "desolate" at the stroke of midnight Sunday, how could the writer know — since the handover hadn't yet occurred — that it would also be "rain-swept"?

This style of writing, increasingly common in newspapers and news magazines, tries too hard. It demonstrates the linguistic intoxication that too often passes for "color" in journalism. Wouldn't it be more natural (by "natural," I mean *better*) to write that China will reclaim Macao from Portugal this weekend, ending 500 years of colonialism for the Macanese?

Here's another drunken lead:

Cooked up to blaze and burn out, igniting a rush that quickly fades into a gnawing need for the next spark, celebrity is the crack cocaine of pop culture.

This, too, is a failed attempt to write colorfully, and it fails because the writer doesn't realize that colorful writing seldom depends upon eccentric phrasing. More often, it depends upon a clear, assertive and emphatic style. Yet, even when the naked point is right before the eye ("Celebrity is the crack cocaine of pop culture"), the writer seems reluctant to highlight it. Instead, he obscures it behind a veil of words: *Cooked up, blazing and burning out, igniting a rush that fades into a gnawing need.* . . .

The following excerpt, again from a large metropolitan daily, is a good candidate for the Bulwer-Lytton contest.

Around the time Buford O. Furrow Jr. allegedly walked into the Jewish community center with an automatic weapon, on a deranged mission that would shock anew this gun-prone and gun-weary land, paramedic Todd Carb was puttering around a firehouse nearby. . . .

Carb was the first firefighter to reach the boy. 'He looked mortally wounded,' Carb said. 'I had doubts he could hold on.'

The rescue of this ebullient child — who was taken off a ventilator Saturday, his condition upgraded from critical to serious — is the stuff of medical expertise flawlessly wielded, of a young life plucked from savagery's foaming maw.

"Savagery's foaming maw," indeed. Start a conversation with that language only if you hope to inspire hoots of laughter.

Clarity and a conversational style are intimate allies that together can tighten and brighten writing. But they bring an equally important and perhaps less obvious benefit: A clear, conversational style can also help make our writing more *sensible.*

11

To catch an eye

Write strong and attractive captions

Studies consistently find that newspaper readers look first at the most eye-catching elements on a page — the big, bright or special elements.

We need studies to tell us this?

Eye-catching, unfortunately for writers, means almost anything but text — headlines, decks, or other enlarged or specialty type; photos and photo captions; art and graphics; design elements such as white space, bullets, and so forth.

Writers often resent the attention given to non-textual elements. They'll fight for every scrap of space to write a longer story. But that's a self-defeating impulse. Writers who know how to be their own best friends will not try to take space from other elements, but will try instead to *make* space for them. They know that those elements will bring the readers into their stories as fat chunks of gray type never will.

Another practice in self-defeat concerns those all-important photo captions. After all, even casual readers visit captions and may or may not read the story based on their attractiveness, readability and interest. Yet captions are often weakly written.

The most common problem in caption writing is pairing a present-tense verb with a past-tense time element. We couldn't say — at least not grammatically — that the new mayor *is* sworn in last week, or that a mother *holds* her son yesterday, or that an officer *carries* a child to safety Wednesday. Yet:

"Lee P. Brown *is* sworn in by U.S. District Judge Vanessa Gilmore to become Houston's mayor Friday."

"Guadalupe Truimo *holds* her 3-year-old son, Jose Marco, while he *is* hooked up to a kidney dialysis machine at Children's Medical Center on *Wednesday*."

"A SWAT team *carries* 7-year-old Jamia Lipscomb to safety *Wednesday* at the end of a nearly 42-hour standoff in McKinney."

Newspaper captions often cook up this sort of sequence-of-tense hash, but there's no reason for it. What keeps us from writing the natural "was sworn in Friday," "held her son Wednesday," "carried Jamia to safety Wednesday"?

This tense problem probably arises because the writer is describing the action in the photo — what is happening in the photo right now. There's nothing wrong with that kind of description, which requires a present-tense verb, unless the caption also contains a past time element, which requires a past-tense verb.

Here are guidelines for avoiding tense problems in captions:

■ When a descriptive sentence includes a past time element, use the simple past:

"Buggies *carried* family and friends to an Amish cemetery in Pembroke, Ky., on *Wednesday* to bury Abram Stoltzfus, 69, killed on Sunday when his buggy was hit by a car driven by a reputed drunken driver."

"Guarded by armed soldiers, Kenyan election workers *continued* counting presidential election ballots *yesterday* in Nairobi, the capital."

"Vice President Al Gore *spoke yesterday* at a rally where Democrats showed their support for President Clinton."

"Defense Secretary William S. Cohen *took* part in a wreath-laying ceremony at the Tomb of the Unknown Soldier in Moscow *yesterday* before talks with the Russian Defense Minister, Igor Sergeyev."

■ Or use the present participle (-ing):

"Lewis C. Fox, a retired Secret Service agent, *leaving* court *yesterday* after being summoned in the Lewinsky matter."

"Al Checchi, a Democratic candidate for governor of California, *directing* a staff meeting *yesterday* at his campaign headquarters in Los Angeles."

■ When a sentence is merely descriptive and includes no time element, use the present tense:

"Gary T. DiCamillo, chief executive of Polaroid, *heads* a new executive group steeped in the ways of the packaged-goods world."

"Jean-Luc Cretier *celebrates* en route to becoming the first Frenchman to win the Olympic downhill since Jean-Claude Killy in 1968."

■ Sometimes you can omit the verb:
"Old haunts: Martin Scorsese in an alley between Lafayette and Mulberry Street."

■ The tense can vary in cutlines with more than one sentence. Time element determines the tense.

"Monica S. Lewinsky *left* her father's home in Los Angeles *yesterday* to return to Washington. Behind her *is* her lawyer, William H. Ginsburg."

"President Suharto *is preparing* for his expected confirmation for a new term next month. He *sat*, center, for an official photograph *yesterday*."

There's more to writing good captions than mechanical accuracy, of course. Their eye-catching visibility demands grace, color and information as well. In other words, once the photo engages the eye, the caption should engage the mind.

And a little personality doesn't hurt, either — witness this pleasing *New York Times* caption, which ran beneath a large color photo and carried the amusing overline "What Next, Locusts?":

"In a spectacular accident in Manhattan yesterday, a century-old water main under Fifth Avenue ruptured, flooding streets and lobbies and gouging out a huge sinkhole that swallowed a car. The shifting asphalt broke a gas main and the gas ignited. No one was injured, but buildings were evacuated and subway service interrupted. The avenue between 19th and 21st Streets was expected to be closed for a week."

Rethinking headlines

Good heads open a door into the story

Once, the newspaper headline was news — it was often the reader's first meeting with a story. From headlines, readers first learned that a fire had destroyed a local theater, or that a nearby store had been robbed, or that the mayor was involved in a scandal. It was the first they heard of it, unless they knew by word-of-mouth. The headline had basically the same purpose as the lead: to reveal at once the story's findings or conclusions.

That principle, although out of date, is still a governing value in writing headlines. A chief criterion of good headline writing is *completeness* — presenting as much of the story as possible in the small space allotted. And the accepted process of writing headlines still focuses on answers rather than questions, on the *what* rather than the *how* or the *why*.

Is that convention still of value? Or — with the proliferation of other, faster media and the increased chance that the readers already know a story's "headline" — has the head's function changed? Is it still to tell the story, or is it a way to get the reader into the story?

If the latter, we must rethink both the purpose of headlines and how we approach them. Headlines that offer the reader a way into the story are usually "open-ended"; they focus on questions instead of answers, thus creating curiosity, interest, mystery. Headlines that shut off reader curiosity and interest are usually "dead-end" headlines — report-writing conclusions that steal a story's "secret." Also, headlines that simply restate the story (or, worse, the *lead*) can make a newspaper seem elemental — repetitive and unsophisticated.

Certain news stories need such heads, even if they report what the reader already knows: "Tornado ravages Wichita; kills 30." But, for example, did John McCain's victory in New Hampshire need a summary head? Convention would say yes, as the following headlines show.

McCain, Gore pick up victories

McCain upsets Bush in New Hampshire primary

McCain big winner over Bush

McCain romps in first primary; Gore wins, Edging Out Bradley

Those headlines simply restate the news and ignore the obvious — the reader already knows it. They are dead-end heads, turning readers away rather than inviting them in. Here's a headline, however, that promises something more:

McCain win in New Hampshire:
'OK, now let's see you do it again'

That intriguing head uses a quote high in the story in which a political commentator said McCain's victory meant nothing unless he could repeat it. The head's forward-looking challenge — "OK, now let's see you do it again" — provokes curiosity and has a conversational and human "voice."

Changing a habit often needs some controlling idea or test to help counter the pressure of convention. In this case, we want to recognize quickly the headline that *must* focus on answers and the headline than *can* focus on questions. One such "test" might be whether the questions *how* or *why* are unintelligible or even ridiculous. Asking why or how a tornado killed 30 in Wichita yields nothing intelligible or promising. But ask why or how or what it means that McCain trounced Bush in New Hampshire, and the questions reveal the story's dimension and richness. As every writer knows, the *facts* of many big stories are quickly dispensed with — they're elemental. The challenging, satisfying and enlightening material lies behind and beyond those facts — in the *how* or *why* rather than the *what*.

If that's true for stories, why not for the headline — the thing we see first and that supposedly sells the story? Consider USA Today's cover story headline: "How the government failed to stop the world's worst Internet attack." Yes, we knew about the attack on university computer systems; what we didn't know was how it happened and why it couldn't be stopped or contained.

The Wall Street Journal excels at creating headlines that "hook" the reader:

Shrewd New Tactics / Help Two Companies / Snare the Top Talent

Never home for dinner? / New Strategies Might / Help You Get There

Analysts Discover Order in the Chaos / Of Huge Valuations for Internet Stocks

Each of those headlines puts enough on the table to provoke curiosity, but not enough to satisfy it. Like the words *how* and *why*, words such as *tactics, strategy, discovery, secret, tips, lessons, keys, mystery, paradox* create interest. They promise to divulge something, and if that something also promises to help the reader in some way, so much the better.

Headlines also intrigue by promising a look inside or behind the scenes — readers naturally want privileged or hidden information. A James Fallows piece in the *Atlantic Monthly* was compellingly titled:

Inside the Leviathan
A short and stimulating brush with Microsoft's corporate culture

A *Smithsonian* story on Intel also had a "look inside" title:

Making the Chips that Run the World
A piece of cake: Put 9 1/2 million transistors in a space the size of your thumbnail and allow zero contamination

Some "look inside" heads from *The Wall Street Journal*:

CacheFlow: The Life Cycle of a Venture-Capital Deal

Tricks of the Web Snoops' Trade

Michael Eisner's New Agenda: Details, Details

The following headlines, from different newspapers but dealing with the same story, show the difference between a dead-end and an open-end headline.

Good headlines invite

German Dax Index Up 1.6 Percent; Others Down Sharply

Success Story in Germany / Is Not All It Appears to Be

The first headline is so complete it shuts off reader curiosity. The second, from *The New York Times*, provokes curiosity with paradox or contradiction.

The main hazard of open-end heads is that the lines are sometimes thin between saying too little, saying enough to interest, and saying so much that interest is satisfied. The mystery that arises from the natural tension of paradox, contradiction, or incongruity is compelling; the mystery that arises from the vague, cryptic or obscure is merely annoying. The question the engaging headline provokes is not a frustrated *What the heck is that supposed to mean?* but an intrigued *Hmm, what's the deal?*

A headline with a question mark is inherently more open and engaging than a statement headline — the former asks; the latter tells. Consider *The Wall Street Journal's* "Is the Awful Behavior of Some Bad Bosses Rooted in Their Past?" That head is more interesting than "Some bosses' bad behavior rooted in past, says study." The question sets us thinking, while the statement seems so simplistic it invites a *duh*.

A question also is safer than a statement when the statement may editorialize. "Are These X-rays Too Revealing?" asks *The Wall Street Journal* over a story dealing with the BodySearch airport screening device. The accompanying photo of a model reveals full details not only of the subject's weapons, but of his nude body. "These X-rays Are Too Revealing!" is hardly objective, while the question allows readers to make the judgment. Other such heads:

AT&T's High Wireless Act: Can it Deliver the Web and a Dial Tone?

Good headlines invite

Can Bob Pittman Make It All Click?

How Would Bush Fare With Foreign Policy? Check out Mexico.

Headlines that are teasingly and pleasingly humorous by virtue of a question mark can become ridiculous without that question mark. "God likes toaster pastries?" asks *USA Today* regarding the television series "God, the Devil and Bob." Imagine that headline rendered: "God likes toaster pastries."

The Wall Street Journal placed this amusing headline on a profile of a man promoting a pastry called *paczki* (pronounced "punchkey"): "Who Put the Paunch in Paczki and Droves in Shrove Tuesday?" The question and word play together make that headline special — and especially inviting. *The Journal* excels at question-cum-word-play heads:

A Hard Question:
Should Church Pews / Be a Comfort Zone?
Tradition: Unpadded Wood; / But Some Devoutly Desire / A Softer Seat of Worship.

Y2 Many Lobsters?
Millennium Revelers / Have Turned Tail
Hoarders Who Bet on a Run / On the Costly Crustaceans / Now Face Being Pinched

Here's the head on a *Journal* story about the Lomo Kompakt Automat, a Soviet-era camera whose images are, in the words of writer Taylor Holliday: "brilliant and bleary, intense and unreliable, enigmatic and mesmerizing all at the same time — kind of like the Soviet era itself, minus the tyranny."

How Lomo Can You Go?

Good headlines invite

The New York Times served up a question-cum-word-play-cum-answer head on a story about television's popular "Who wants to be a millionaire?"

Who Wants to Be Retro? Multimillions

And here's *The Wall Street Journal's* treatment of the sudden rash of new quiz shows:

An Overdose of Quizzes? No Question

The *Journal* also used a question to make the most of a headline on a story reviewing reactions to the AOL-Time Warner merger: "This Changes Everything! Or Does It?"

Although questions quickly and easily provoke reader interest and curiosity, we can't litter headline space with question marks, valuable as they are. Heads that focus on the *how* or the *why* or the *what now* accomplish the same end — often without asking a direct question. *The Wall Street Journal* consistently offers great *how* and *why* headlines:

How a Single Sentence by IRS Paved the Way to Cash-Balance Plans

How Market Slumps Alter Psychology

How Steve Case Morphed Into a Media Mogul

How a Need for Speed Turned Guadalajara Into a High-Tech Hub

How a Ballpark Tip Evolved Into a Burden for One of the Big Five

How Did Stores Do This Season? Two Syllables: Ka-Ching!

Good headlines invite

How the GOP Faithful Forged a Golden Chain
Behind Bush Campaign

Why a Firefighter Needs a Garden Hose to Do His Thing

What now headlines are questions with or without question marks — they point to the future rather than to the past and emphasize the unknown rather than the known:

The American Century: Is It Going or Coming? (WSJ)

As Gasoline Prices Rise, the Cost of New Cars and Trucks May Fall
(NYT)

Toys 'R' Us Hires F.A.O. Chief, Hoping to Coax Back Customers
(NYT)

He Engineered a Mob Hit, and Now It's Time to Pay Up
Entering a 2nd Season, 'The Sopranos' Has a Hard Act to Follow
(NYT)

Headline writers could take a crash course in what catches the reader's eye by studying the covers of popular magazines. Here are lines from a handful of recent *Time* covers:

How to Save the Earth

Testosterone: Is the Edge worth It?

How to Improve Your Memory

The Hottest Jobs of the Future

Good headlines invite

Inside a Hacker School

The Truth About Bankruptcy

The Love Bug: How it Works. How to Protect Yourself Against Viruses

The Future of Technology:
Smart Cars, Uppity Robots and Cybersex. Are you ready?

Language myths hinder graceful writing

Wordsmiths split hairs on infinitives, verbs

Linguistic and grammatical myths sometimes get in the way of graceful prose and good editing. We commonly hear, for example, that the word *none* is always singular. It isn't, as any number of respected reference works will testify. The word can mean "no few" or "no several" as well as "no one." And this is nothing new; *none* has been used with both singular and plural verbs for many centuries.

But we've heard somewhere that *none* is always singular, so we believe it. We don't question the myth; we don't investigate. Instead, we genuflect before the irrational and create monstrosities such as "none of the people *is* pleased with the outcome." And although that diction offends both the ear and common sense, we're satisfied because we've followed some imaginary rule.

The language is not as perverse as we're willing to believe. Rules and traditions promote accuracy, clarity and grace. They solve rather than create problems. When a "rule" results in the unnatural, ambiguous or ugly, we should look it up. The chances are good we'll find no such rule exists. Then we — writers, editors and educators alike — can stop parroting and perpetuating linguistic nonsense. At the very least, since words are our business, we should also make it our business to know a little more about them.

Here's another commonly held but mistaken notion: It's wrong to split infinitives. In the 1800s, Latin was the model for good writing, and wordsmiths tried to make English conform to Latin. The attempt was impractical where infinitives were concerned because the infinitive in Latin is one word and *cannot* be split. On the other hand, we occasionally *must* split the infinitive in English.

The most we can say about split infinitives — and it should be enough to keep us from splitting them willy nilly — is that they're often awkward and unattractive. But they're not wrong.

Nothing about a split infinitive makes it desirable in itself. But, as H. W. Fowler writes, it is preferable to real ambiguity or patent artificiality. We should feel perfectly free to split an infinitive when the unsplit version is clumsy or unclear. "We wanted to immediately leave for the airport" splits an infinitive and is the worse for it. But try unsplitting the following sentences, and see the resulting distortion, error or ambiguity that results:

"Administrators expect profits to *more than* triple this year."

"The committee plans to *legally* ban frank disclosures."

"We hope to *strongly* protest advancing the proposal."

Those examples make it clear that a split infinitive is sometimes not only permissible, but necessary.

While the notion that split infinitives are wrong has wide currency, another language myth seems perpetuated chiefly by the journalistic community. That's the odd and insupportable practice of unsplitting perfectly clear and natural split compound verbs (*should probably go, will never be*). Like the split infinitive, the split verb phrase is not an error. Good writers and speakers split them all the time.

Obviously, we should avoid awkward splits. *"He drove the car* that I *had last year given* to my cousin" should be "the car that I had given to my cousin last year." But "the proposal was tentatively approved" is just fine — better, in fact, than "the proposal tentatively was approved," or "the proposal was approved tentatively."

Here's a handful of split verbs from good writers. All are fine as they stand, and some are better as they stand than if unsplit.

Marshall Frady: Clinton *was also confronted* with the decision on whether to allow the execution. . . . The matter of Ricky Rector *could hardly have seemed* a more incidental concern in the political havoc surrounding Clinton at that moment.

Jamaica Kincaid: I accept that I now live in a climate that has four seasons, one of which I *do not fully appreciate.*

Vikram Seth: Many people *were literally squeezed* to death upright against each other.

Ken Auletta: Their names *were immediately filed* in his PowerBook.

William Trevor: They were in their sixties and *had scarcely parted* from each other in the forty-two years of their marriage.

Terrence Rafferty: Rodriguez's grubby little thriller has generated a nice buzz on the film-festival circuit. . . and it's *now being distributed* by a major studio.

John Lahr: Now that history has put paid to the delirium of ideology, Rattigan's intelligence and quiet audacity *are more easily seen.*

Katha Pollitt: I *was once invited* to contribute to an anthology about potatoes. . . .

Those sentences are excerpted from the *New Yorker,* but we could find them anywhere. Trust me: There's a whole literate world out there that has never even *heard* of the "problem" of the split verb. In this as in all regards, the practice of good editing should be to make writing better without making it worse.

15

Grammatically speaking

Writers should avoid polluting the language environment

Grammar and usage problems abound in media writing as they do elsewhere. But professional writers should avoid the snares of common language traps. Here are some of the peskiest perennials.

■ Pronouns constantly bring writers and speakers to grief. "She's older than *him*," we read or hear. "They gave the reports to Smith, Jones and *myself*." "This is between you and *I*." Common as such ungrammatical statements are, handling pronouns isn't difficult. The choice of pronoun depends upon whether the word is a subject or object. If it's a subject, it acts: *I, he, she, they, we, who,* for example. And if it's an object, it receives the action: *me, him, her, them, us, whom,* for example. "Self" pronouns are not subjects or objects but reflexives (*I* hurt *myself*) or intensifiers (*they* all think something, but *I myself* think otherwise).

"She's older than *him*," actually says "she's older than *he is*," so we need the subject *he* for the verb *is* — even though *is* isn't spoken. (We would not say, "She's older than *him* is," so *him* would be the wrong choice.)

If we remove "Smith and Jones" from "they gave the reports to Smith, Jones and myself," we'll see right away that we need a simple object: Not "they gave the reports to *myself*," but "they gave the reports to *me*."

We can substitute another pronoun in such sentences as "this is between you and *I*." Remove *you and I* and use other pronouns: "This is between *we*; this is between *us*." Again, we see immediately that *between we* is wrong and *between us* is right. So we'd need the objective pronoun in all cases: "This is between you and *me*."

■ The substitution game also is useful in settling *who/whom* questions. (*Who* is the subject, *whom* the object.) Nobody has a problem with, "Who called?" But change that sentence to "who *did you say* called," and many want to make it *whom*. Yet it's the same sort of sentence — it says: *You did say she, he, they called*. Again, those pronouns *she, he, they* show that we need a subject (*who*), not an object — we would not say *you said him called*.

One of the hardest *who* problem is in such sentences as: "They planned to confront *whoever/whomever* distributed the leaflets." The correct choice is *whoever*, although many would choose *whomever*. Such sentences are confusing because we want an object for *confront*, yet we need a subject for *distributed*. In such sentences, the subjective pronoun always wins. And the whole clause *whoever distributed the leaflets* serves as the object for *confront*.

■ "Agreement" problems plague American writers and speakers. Consider: "She's one of those people who always tries to get everything right." *Tries* is wrong here; the writer is making it agree with *one*, but the subject for the verb *try* is *who*, which in turn refers to *people*. This sentence says: *Of the people who always try to get everything right, she is one*.

Here's another agreement problem in action: "A banking commercial on TV asks the viewing audience if they're beginning to feel like a number rather than a person." Here, the singular collective noun *audience* is followed by the plural *they're*, which doesn't agree in number with "audience," "a number," or "a person." The easiest correction is: "A banking commercial on TV asks the *viewers* if they're beginning to feel like *numbers* rather than *people*." We could change *viewers* to *viewer*, and it would agree with "a number" or "a person." But then we'd have the troubling gender problem. Should we follow the traditional practice of treating the masculine pronoun as neuter and use *he*? We should not. Should we use *he or she*? We should not. The best solution to gender problems is to make the antecedent plural. "Any *employee* wishing to change *his* benefits plan. . . ." could read: "*employees* wishing to change *their* benefits plans. . . ."

Collective nouns (*class, group, family, committee, company*, etc.) are usually singular in American English. "The Acme *Company* will move *their* warehouse to *their* new location in June" should say "*its* warehouse to *its* new location." (But never, ever *it's*, which is not possessive and means *it is*.) *Anyone, anybody, no one, nobody, everyone*, and *everybody* also are singular. "*Anyone* who thinks *they* could be a professional golfer should talk to me" should be recast to fix the agreement problem: "Golfers who think they could be professional should talk to me."

■ *What* clauses, a tired favorite of media writers, often create agreement problems: "He said he objected to what seems to be desperate attempts to sabotage the project." *What* can be either singular or plural, depending upon the sentence. Here, the what refers to *attempts*, so the verb should be *seem*, not *seems*. If the *what* referred to one attempt, however, *seems* would be correct.

■ The subjunctive *were* also creates grammar problems for many writers: "If it was up to Sandra Eberling, no child would go to bed hungry." This sentence is contrary to fact (it's *not* up to Sandra Eberling), so should read: "If it *were* up to Sandra Eberling. . . ." Use *were* with "if" structures that express wish or desire or are contrary to fact: If I *were* queen; I wish you *were* going; he says that if he *were* president. . . . Some writers overcorrect and use *were* with all "if" sentences: "I wondered if he *were* president." That's equally wrong — the sentence is simple past tense, not subjunctive.

Pronoun, agreement and subjunctive mood problems are just several of the problems facing writers, but together they make up a large part of the pollution clouding our communications. If we handle those problems with greater proficiency, the linguistic environment would get cleaner overnight.

Pet peeves

Go ahead, ax me about irregardless

Most people are passionate about what they consider misuse of the language. One seldom hears such mild reproofs as: *Oh, my goodness, his grammar is a bit off-putting.* Or: *My, her pronunciation is quaint, isn't it?*

No. We hear instead: *If he says 'irregardless' again, I'm going to shoot him.* Or: *If she doesn't stop saying 'ax' instead of 'ask,' I'm going to throw something.*

Our metaphors for language misuse are often violent. We don't say people misuse the language; we say they "maim," "abuse," "massacre," "brutalize" or "butcher" it. That visceral reaction probably arises in part because our language and our ideas of its proper use are dear to us. A native tongue is of great value to its speakers, who are sensitive to its use even if they themselves are not expert users. Some countries even have ministries of language charged with preserving the purity of the mother tongue.

Maybe that sensitivity is why we so often feel bound to correct others' grammar or usage although we know it might embarrass them. Even if we don't correct, the temptation to do so is strong — sometimes almost a reflex. Let someone say "This is between you and I," and someone else blurts almost without thinking: "between you and *me*."

Whatever the reason, most people have well-defined linguistic pet peeves. Occasionally, to be sure, the person with the peeve is wrong — as is the case with the supposed "errors" of the split infinitive, ending sentences with prepositions, using *couple* or *none* as plural nouns, or beginning sentences with *and* or *but*. Not one of those is a mistake, according to language experts, but folks who wrongly think so are no less peeved for being wrong. Instead, they usually respond: "Well, OK, it may not be a mistake, but I still don't like it!"

It's hard to give up a peeve, especially a pet one.

Some of the strongest peeves have to do with speech rather than writing. Many cannot bear to hear the word *nuclear* pronounced "nucular," or *Realtor* pronounced "realator." Others are driven crazy by double negatives such as *can't hardly, don't have no, can't do nothing*. Still others go crazy over the repeated use of *you know* or *totally*.

I recently saw a roomful of editors flinch when they heard someone use "antidote" when he meant *anecdote*. A colleague says that when he hears *literally* and *figuratively* confused, he stops in his figurative tracks and grits his literal teeth. On my own list of teeth-grinding grotesqueries are "ekcetera" instead of *etcetera*, and "asterick" instead of *asterisk*.

Many people can hardly bear the gratuitous suffix "-wise" tacked onto nouns. They have plenty of opportunity to exercise their peeve — one hears that leaden, lengthening syllable everywhere. I recently arrived at a banquet hall to deliver a speech on linguistic grace and precision, and the host announced they were having trouble "microphonewise." The trendy "-wise" habit is nothing new — Jack Lemmon angrily remarked to jargon-spouting colleagues in an old movie I've otherwise forgotten: "And that's the way it crumbles, cookiewise!"

Those who dislike "-wise" are usually equally disgusted with "ize." "Utilize" is an outcast in the land of the peeved. "Incentivize," meaning to provide incentives, is a more recent "ize" creation — along with "strategize," "conceptualize," "finalize" and "optimize." Edwin Newman writes in *A Civil Tongue* of a television news anchor who said that a slain deputy sheriff would be "funeral-ized" the next day.

Misunderstood expressions also can annoy. An acquaintance sets everyone's teeth on edge when he says "six of one and a dozen of the other." Another common peeve is the expression "I could care less" rather than "I *couldn't* care less." (If you *could* care *less*, then you care somewhat. But if you could *not* care less, then you don't care at all.)

Being sensitive to the language and scornful of its misuse is nothing new. Long ago, the Latin word *balbus* meant someone who stammered or spoke haltingly. That word passed into Spanish as *bobo* and in turn spawned *booby* or *boob*. And just as we mimic incomprehensible language with the words *blah blah*, the Greeks made fun of what they considered gibberish with the words *bar-bar*. The Greeks were proud of their language, as we all are, and were scornful of those who did not know it. Eventually *bar-bar* came to mean foreign or savage and in time transmuted to *barbaros* and the related *barbarous, barbarism* and *barbarian*.

It's both interesting and significant that those words, which mean *uncivilized*, can be traced to a lack of fluency. Apparently, our inherent understanding of being civilized means, in part, the ability to communicate well — not only with grace and accuracy, but without offense.

Spell-checkers

Don't jump to conclusions when playing with checkers

The chief danger of depending on a computer's spell-checker is well-known. The software is good at flagging misspelled or repeated words but can't distinguish among homophones such as *there, their,* and *they're,* or *to, two* and *too.*

But if spell-checkers are risky, grammar-checkers are downright dangerous. My grammar software, for example spits up so many grammatical hairballs that you'd think swallowing those grammar rules had served only to give it indigestion.

Like the spell-checker, though, grammar software has several strengths. It's good at flagging long sequences of noun modifiers, for example. It suggests revising "several state air control board members" and gags on "television quiz show letter-turner Vanna White." It also catches many *that* and *which* errors. Responding to "The board has approved a plan *which* will create a more effective enforcement program," the checker correctly suggests: "Consider using *that* as the restrictive relative pronoun." It also dependably flags overused or frequently misused expressions such as *basically, in fact,* or *literally.*

But many of the checker's suggestions are wrong — some so wrong they amuse. Write: "How much of the following sentence do you understand?" and the grammar-checker suggests using *does* instead of *do*. Oddly, while recommending "*does* you understand," it balks at "you be the judge." *You be* is, of course, a substandard substitute for you are, but it's not ungrammatical in *you be the judge*.

Such pesky exceptions baffle the grammar-checker. Write "deemed suitable," and it says to consider *suitably* instead. It doesn't know that the rules governing, say, *ran swiftly* don't apply to *deemed suitable*. Linguistic rote inevitably causes problems for the checker – witness its following unhelpful responses:

Original: "Brevity and clarity are companions."

Grammar Checker: "The word *clarity* does not agree with *are*. Consider *is* instead of *are*."

Original: "Blitz comes from *blitzkrieg*, which means, literally, 'lightning war.'"

GC: "Consider *lightening* instead of *lightning*."

Original: "Having the screaming meemies is like having the heebie-jeebies."

GC: "Consider *as* or *as if* instead of *like*."

Original: "Adlai Stevenson feared that Secretary of State John Foster Dulles' hard-line tactics were taking us to the brink of war."

GC: "*Were* does not agree with *secretary*. Consider *was*."

Original: "He termed Dulles' approach *brinkmanship*, a term now used to identify risky negotiation."

GC: "This appears to be a run-on sentence."

Original: "We have so many war words that lexicographers have created whole books of them."

GC: "The word *many* does not agree with *war*. Consider *wars*." (Amusingly, when I ran this completed column through the checker, it flagged the previous sentence – its *own* sentence – and remarked: "The word *many* does not agree with *does*. Consider *do* instead of *does*.")

Spell-checkers

Some grammar-checker problems have to do with punctuation – such as its incoherent suggestion that we substitute "double dashes" for "single dashes." It's true that we once were forced to use two hyphens when we needed a dash, but that was because "typewriter" technology provided no dash. The practice was a compromise, not a preference, and where dashes are available, we should use them.

Many checker problems arise from the old-fashioned idea that *formal* writing is preferable to *informal* writing, a spurious notion responsible for much of the poor writing we see in business, academe and the professions. What might "informal" writing be, in any case — slang or profanity or cursive script and little hearts dotting the i's? That certainly would be informal, but no professional would do such things, anyway. Fact is, we *need* the warmth, voice, humanity and conversational style that informality brings. Formality's stiffness, pretension, jargon and lack of humanity damage writing wherever they appear.

The checker's archaic and arbitrary dictum against contractions is an example of this formal/informal nonsense. It wants all contractions written out. Write: "If you couldn't or wouldn't say it, don't write it," and the checker offers this stiffer version: "If you could not or would not say it, do not write it." But contractions are both graceful and conversational, and we should use them whenever they sound better than writing out the words.

The checker holds still other old-fashioned ideas – such as the "error" of starting a sentence with *and* or *but* or ending it with a preposition. Consider the last sentence in the preceding paragraph ("*But* contractions are both graceful and conversational. . . .") and this one: "It wants all contractions written *out*."

Are those sentences wrong?

You be the judge.

Spell-checkers

The grammar-checker's shortcomings recall the truism that to create artificial intelligence, it takes the real thing. The human brain, with its flexibility and capacity to imagine, is still superior in many ways to the electronic model. The computer is never tired or preoccupied or careless, so it is wonderful at remembering and observing rules. But it doesn't have the imagination of even a very young human brain — which not only can forget the rules, but can find in them loopholes and options. Electronic intelligence can process information like a house afire, but it still can't *think*.

18 & 19

Notes on usage

Accepted and traditional definitions are the safest

William Safire was correct when he said about word use: "When enough of us are wrong, we're right." Words must mean what most educated readers think they mean. Definitions are not set in stone. Perceptions change and, over time, some words change to match that perception.

However, professional writers and editors — especially professionals working for a mass medium — should avoid using words that are in transition or are otherwise controversial. Such use may reflect badly on their linguistic skill, thus alienating knowledgeable readers by seeming to cheapen the language. The most sensible course is to follow the accepted (also called the *standard* or *preferred*) meaning of a word.

Following are commonly misused or misunderstood words and expressions. A few of these are words in transition — *moot point*, for example, which is gradually losing its centuries-old meaning of "debatable" and assuming a new identity as "academic" or "irrelevant." Its primary meaning is still "debatable," but its definition is changing, making it a poor choice for a mass medium. If a word is in transition from one definition to another and possibly misunderstood whichever definition we choose, the sensible path is to avoid the word. We have plenty of others — the huge lexicon of English is rich in synonym and near-synonym.

In any case, words in transition are invariably faddish and over-used and bring neither originality nor precision. A fad-free vocabulary avoids offense and is fresher, more pointed and concrete. ("Debatable" causes no problem, for example. Neither does "academic" or "irrelevant." Those words, then, are better choices than the more trendy "moot point.")

There's no reason to avoid words and expressions that are often misused but aren't *changing*, however. We should simply use them correctly. ("Moot point," for example, is sometimes rendered "*mute* point." That's just wrong.)

Everyone makes mistakes. But writers and editors should know as much as possible about the language and sidestep problems that get in the way of the message. Why bother defending questionable usage? Again, there's always a better — and uncontroversial — choice. The weakest defense for shoddy usage is "lots of people use the word [or expression] that way." Lots of people have only the most tenuous grasp of literacy, come to that, and therefore shouldn't be models for professional writers. It's a matter of pride and taste.

A dictionary often is not the best guide in usage. Dictionaries are wonderful, but they're basically descriptive rather than *prescriptive*; their job is to tell us what *is*, not what should be — they present *diction*. Many substandard words are in the dictionary; a good dictionary would be remiss not to include them. But they're not always so labeled.

And dictionaries differ. Some are more permissive than others. (The Associated Press' chosen dictionary, Webster's New World, is relatively permissive.) The front pages of a dictionary reveal its philosophy as well as how it works.

Again, what dictionary committees refer to as "preferred" meanings are the most common, accepted or primary meanings. That doesn't mean all definitions are equal, just that it's a dictionary's job to present all probable definitions of a word. Even the best dictionaries can't provide usage notes for every entry that needs it. Therefore, a good usage reference should be part of every writer's library. One of the best is Theodore Bernstein's *The Careful Writer* (Atheneum). It's out of print, but you may be able to find a copy. Wilson Follet's *Modern American Usage* is helpful; so is John Bremner's *Words on Words*.

I consulted a variety of works in compiling this list. Webster's New World Dictionary settled disputes — not because it is superior, but because it's the arbiter for the AP.

AS. Strike the *as* from: "was named (or *chosen* or *elected*) as president, successor, chairman." This is like saying: "They named their new baby *as* Tiffany." Also, strike *as* from the ungrammatical "equally *as*."

AS TO, AS TO WHETHER. Avoid this gobbledygook. Example: "As to whether Anderson has eclipsed Duchovny, he refused to touch on the issue. . . ." *Better:* "He wouldn't discuss whether Anderson has eclipsed Duchovny."

BEGS THE QUESTION doesn't mean to provoke the question or that the question arises. It's a term of logic meaning to *offer as evidence the very thing you're trying to prove.* If, for example, I argue that the Holy Bible is inspired and, as evidence, I offer biblical scripture saying it is inspired, I am begging the question. Or: I argue that two parallel lines will never meet because they are parallel.

COHORT best identifies a group of people, each of whom has something specific in common. The birth cohort of 1946. The cohort of baby boomers. From Theodore Bernstein's *The Careful Writer*: "The misuse of *cohort* to denote an individual is common.... This misuse can result only from bad guessing. Having in mind such words as *costar, coauthor,* and *cotrustee,* in which the prefix 'co-' has the meaning of 'with,' the bad guesser apparently decides that a cohort is a *hort* who is co- with another *hort.* And what is a *hort?* That they don't bother to find out. Actually the 'co-' in *cohort* is not a prefix at all. The word comes from a Latin word meaning an enclosure. It was originally applied to a division in the Roman army, and now means a company or band, as in 'a cohort of Yale students.'"

COMPARE. *Compare* deals both with likes and unlikes, similarities and contrasts. When referring only to similarities, *liken* is the better word. "Hitchcock compared her to an ice princess" is better rendered "*likened* her to an ice princess" because it involves no actual comparison.

COMPRISE does not mean *consist of* or *constitute.* It means to include or contain and is used in the way those words are used. The whole *comprises* the parts. The whole *consists of* the parts. The parts *constitute* the whole. This is a nation *comprising* 50 states. That set of history books *comprises* 30 volumes.

"Comprise *of*" is always wrong.

CONVINCE/PERSUADE. We convince *of* or *that,* but persuade *to.* From Bernstein's *Careful Writer*: "*Persuade* is sometimes followed by an infinitive, whereas *convince* never is."

DECIMATE does not mean widespread destruction. It means to destroy a small part — a tenth, to be exact. Like many words beginning with the prefix *dec* (decade, decimal), *decimate* pertains to ten. Nobody's going to insist on that ten percent, but *fractional* is a far cry from *total* or even *most*.

Note: Don't qualify *decimate: completely, rather, somewhat* decimated.

DÉJA VU does not mean a repeated occurrence or experience. The expression refers to a momentary illusion that something has happened before *when it has not.*

DILEMMA. A dilemma is not a simple problem or quandary. It's a predicament — a situation in which one must choose between two *unattractive* options. Hence the expression "caught on the horns of a dilemma."

DISINTERESTED means objective or unbiased, not bored or indifferent. The word for the latter is *uninterested.*

DISSOCIATE is the preferred pronunciation and spelling, not "disassociate."

DOVE. The past tense of *dive* is *dived.*

ERGO, E.G., I.E. *Ergo* means "therefore," *e.g.* comes from *exempli gratia*, which means "for example," and *i.e.* comes from *id est*, which means "that is" or "that is to say." Latinisms once were common in prose because readers usually were schooled in Latin — but that's no longer the case, and some see their use as pretentious. In any case, these terms seem less appropriate for media use than *therefore, for example* and *that is.*

ENORMITY. This word has provoked controversy for years. Everyone agrees that *enormity* means "wicked" or "odious," but some don't *want* it to mean that. Whatever, "enormity" carries a meaning that "enormousness" lacks, so the word is a problem that we should avoid if we're referring only to size or scope — without the extra dimension of wickedness. The enormity of Hitler's crimes, but the size, scope or enormousness of Van Gogh's artistry.

ENTHUSE is a verb, not an adjective. ("I'm *enthusiastic* about my new job," she *enthused*. Not: "I'm *enthused* about my new job.") The verb *enthuse* is a back formation of the noun *enthusiasm*, and while it has gained in legitimacy, it's still seen as colloquial. *Enthuse* as an adjective, however, is simply wrong; the adjective is *enthusiastic*.

EPITOME does not mean the highest or best form. It means abridgment, abstract or summary. A person or thing that epitomizes something captures the essence or typical qualities of that something. It's an embodiment, not an *ideal*.

EXCEPTION PROVES THE RULE. How can the exception prove the rule? Easy: it doesn't. The problem here is that *prove* once meant *test*. We see this sense in two other old expressions, *proving ground* (testing ground) and *the proof of the pudding is in the eating* (the test of the pudding.) A "proofing oven" is a testing oven: dough rises there until we test it to see if it's ready for baking. So "the exception proves the rule" really means that the exception *tests* the rule.

By the way, we sometimes hear or read: "The proof is in the pudding." That expression is as weird as it is incorrect.

FORTHCOMING does not mean forthright. *Forthcoming* means coming forth, about to appear, available or ready when needed. When we mean candid, direct or straightforward, we mean *forthright*. This word is consistently misused in the media.

FORTUITOUS does not mean fortunate. It means accidental, happening by chance. If a fortuitous event is also fortunate, so much the better. Many aren't.

FRACTIOUS, FACTIOUS. The newly faddish *fractious* is often misused in the media. *Fractious* simply means unruly or disorderly — it has nothing to do with fractions or factions. *Factious* is the word that relates to factions, so it is usually factiousness (not *fractiousness*) that describes divisive dissent.

FULSOME does not mean lavish or abundant. *Fulsome* means disgusting or offensive (often because insincere). The critic who wrote that a production deserved "fulsome praise" wrote something strange indeed.

GAMUT, GANTLET, GAUNTLET. We run the gamut or gantlet, but throw down the gauntlet. "Running the gauntlet" is a misuse — *gauntlet* means a glove, and throwing it down means to issue a challenge (once, to challenge to a duel).

A *gantlet* was originally a military punishment in which the victim had to run between two rows of people who beat him.

A *gamut*, in music, is a series of musical notes or scale.

GRADUATED needs the preposition *from*. Avoid "graduated college," or the like.

HAVE A TEMPERATURE. We always have a temperature. If that temperature rises above normal, we have a *fever*.

HAVE ONE'S CAKE AND EAT IT, TOO. An illogical expression that should be wanting to "*eat* one's cake and *have* it, too." That's the only way the expression makes sense. We must always *have* our cake before we eat it. The expression is meaningful only in wanting to *eat* our cake and then *still* to have it — in that order. Such a desire is unreasonable, which is what the expression suggests.

HOBSON'S CHOICE does not mean a quandary, dilemma or difficult choice — it means no choice at all. Thomas Hobson, a liveryman in England several hundred years ago, had a rule that customers must "choose" the horse nearest the stable door — thus, the customer had *no* choice.

HYPE. *Hype* is pejorative. It means to inflate or exaggerate the worth of, even to deceive.

Hype is defined: to trick, gull, swindle or deceive; to promote or publicize showily, often by questionable methods. Hyping suggests dishonesty, so we shouldn't write that people are hyping something when all they're doing is promoting or publicizing or selling. Use *promote, sell, publicize, publicity* or some equivalent word.

IMPLY, INFER. The common error: "Are you inferring that I'm. . . ." A speaker or writer cannot infer or make inferences; the listener or reader makes inferences. The speaker *implies*, and the audience *infers* from the speaker's implication.

JUST DESERTS is not so much misused as it is misunderstood and misspelled. The expression has nothing to do with dessert; it means, as we suppose, to get what one justly deserves. *Deserts* derives from a French root meaning to *deserve*, and it has a single "S."

LIKELY is not a synonym for probably. *Likely* is an adjective, parallel to the adjective *probable* rather than to the adverb *probably*. (Not all words ending with LY are adverbs.)

Therefore, *likely* behaves like an adjective, with a "be" verb usually preceding: *The situation is likely to worsen.* Not: *The situation likely will worsen.* (Exception: This rule does not apply when the superlatives *very* or *most* precede *likely*.)

Awkward: They likely will win.

Better: They are likely to win.

Or: They probably will win.

OK: They most likely will win.

LITANY does not mean a mere list. It's a prayer or repetitive chant and means something overlong, droning or repetitive.

MOOT. The word's traditional and still preferred meaning is *debatable*, but *moot* is moving steadily toward meaning *irrelevant*. Best avoided. Use *debatable, irrelevant, academic, null . . .*

MYRIAD, the noun (*a myriad of*) does not mean *many* — it means 10,000. We usually want the adjective *myriad*, which means many (*I have myriad reasons*).

NAUSEOUS does not mean nauseated. *Nauseous* is an adjective meaning sickening or disgusting. As is often said: If we're nauseated, *we're* sick; if we're nauseous, we make *others* sick.

NOTORIETY does not mean of note or fame. This pejorative word is related to *notorious*, not *noted*. A stage star might be *noted* for his acting skill but *notorious* for his temper tantrums.

PODIUM does not mean lectern. We stand on the *podium*, but speak at or behind the *lectern*. *Lectern* is related to *lecture; podium* to the Greek and Latin roots for foot, *pod* and *ped*.

PRESENTLY does not mean *now*. It means soon. *Now* is a good word when we mean now, and *currently* will do if we're enchanted with unnecessary syllables.

PRONE, SUPINE. *Supine* means face up, *prone* face down. The columnist who wrote that she had spent the morning lying prone in the dentist's chair had the wrong doctor.

RETICENT means silent or reluctant to *speak*. The word does not signify reluctance to do anything else.

SANK, SUNK. Sank stands alone; *sunk* needs a helping verb: *is, was, are, were, am, have, had* sunk.

SCENARIO doesn't mean scene or vignette. It's a complete script: beginning, middle, end.

SINGLE MOST, SINGLE BEST, SINGLE BIGGEST. *Single* can't modify those superlatives. Put the word in front of what it *does* modify (best single day, biggest single donation). Or strike it.

SNUCK. Ungrammatical. *Sneaked.*

SYMPATHY, EMPATHY. These words are getting fuzzed up in general use, but the distinction between them is worth preserving. To *empathize* means to deeply understand, even identify with, another's feelings. To *sympathize* means simply to feel compassion or pity.

THAT. Some journalists habitually and wrongly delete this valuable word, thus creating some unclear or odd sentences:

1) "The chairman said yesterday Smith resigned." Use *that* when a time element comes between verb and clause. ("The chairman said yesterday *that* Smith resigned," or "The chairman said *that* yesterday Smith resigned.")

2) "The committee proposed a policy members can approve." Use *that* when the clause is in apposition to a noun. ("The committee proposed a policy *that* members can approve.")

3) "The mayor revealed the findings of a confidential report had been leaked to the press." Use *that* when the verb of the clause is delayed. Without a *that* after "revealed," the readers don't know that *findings* is the subject of a clause and will at first assume that the mayor revealed the findings rather than the leak.

THESE, THOSE. In careful writing, *those* refers to something in the preceding passage, *these* to the current or following passage.

UNIQUE cannot be modified (*very, really, completely* unique). It means "one of a kind" and stands alone.

VERBAL AGREEMENT does not mean *oral* agreement. *Verbal* means words, both written and spoken. All agreements are at least verbal (unless we're consigned to grunts). Use *oral* or *spoken* agreement.

WHAT, WHICH. *What* is often misused as a substitute for *which*. Examples: "She knows *what* foods have a high fat content"; "decide *what* course to take. . ." The *what* should be *which* in such cases.

Solving the Ambrose Bierce mystery

Why do people want to put a straitjacket on the language?

Proactive, a newly-minted word (or non-word, as many would have it), is not in the latest *Oxford Dictionary of New Words*. That dictionary, published in 1991 and now out in paperback, lists 2,000 words and meanings that have become popular in the last decade.

At the moment, *proactive* is among the most *and* least popular new words in the United States. Yet, even though most of us have heard the word and either embraced or rejected it, its adoption into popular culture is so recent that it's neither on a recent list of new words nor in most commonly used dictionaries. (Of the nine dictionaries I consulted, I found *proactive* only in the 1991 edition of *Webster's College Dictionary* from Random House and in the 1983 edition of *Webster's Ninth New Collegiate*. The older volume, however, defines the word in a way unlike the way we now use it. It also traces it to the '30s, thus we surmise that *proactive* had another life and identity before this more recent incarnation.)

However frowned upon it may be, *proactive* will be recognized and defined by dictionaries if it remains in use. That's the dictionary's job. But for now, we must guess at its meaning. In current contexts, it seems to mean the opposite of "reactive." Of course, if that is the intent, a better word would be "preactive." But never mind. For good or ill, the language has opened its arms to *proactive*, so *proactive* it is.

This whole business with *proactive* shows how quickly a new word or meaning can travel through the language. It also shows that the language has a mind of its own. It changes despite our efforts to make it stay the same, and it stays the same despite our efforts to change it. Its ardor in embracing the new is equal only to its fierceness in resisting it.

We can readily see these two faces of the language in the work of grammarians from other eras. Ambrose Bierce's century-old list of incorrectly used words, for example, contains many of today's incorrectly used words as well. But other words on Bierce's list have long since completed their journey from one definition to another, and it's news to us that they ever had another meaning.

Ambrose Bierce was a respected writer and editor in the late 1800s and early 1900s — although he may be better known for his mysterious disappearance in Mexico. Before he vanished, though, Bierce was for decades a fierce spokesman for the purity of the language. He wanted words to be carefully and clearly defined and then to be used accordingly. Forever, I guess. Otherwise, he said, precise communication was impossible.

And precise communication *would* be impossible if most or even many words were unstable at the same time. But only a tiny fraction of the English lexicon is changing at a given moment.

In Bierce's day, the expression "the price of admission" was considered incorrect. The correct form was thought to be "the price of *admittance*." But now we routinely use the word *admission*, and no one considers it a problem.

Bierce and his contemporaries also fussed about the phrasing *build* a fire or *build* a canal or *build* a tunnel. You can't *build* fires and canals and tunnels, they protested. You have to *make* a fire and *dig* canals and tunnels. Well, their logic was impeccable. Yet today we say "build a fire" and give no thought to the logic or illogic of the expression.

Another irritant a century ago was the loss of the past tense for such words as *bet, wet, knit* and *quit.* Bierce grouched that, after all, those were regular verbs and their past tenses should be *betted, wetted, knitted* and *quitted.* He lost that battle, too, because of those forms the only one we still use is *knitted,* and that inconsistently. For the rest, we say: he bet on the horses last week, they wet down the field, she quit her job.

Bierce also complained about the habit of using "dirt" when one meant soil or earth or ground, a habit we practice today. He called that usage a "most disagreeable Americanism" and reminded his readers that *dirt* meant *filth.* That's another fight he lost.

But we're in agreement with some of Bierce's other gripes — using the word *human* as a noun, for example. *Human* is an adjective, he explained, so we should call people human *beings* and not *humans.* Interestingly, we still see *human* standing alone as graceless if not incorrect, so even a hundred years of misuse has not forced us to accept the word *human* as a noun.

Bierce wrote that such words as *authoress* and *poetess* were unnecessary. And we still say so. He pointed out that there was no such word as *doubtlessly* because *doubtless* says it all. And we agree, a hundred years later. He said the expression *equally as* (as in equally as good or equally as tall) was ungrammatical. And it still is. (Equally good or equally tall are the correct forms.) He complained that "feel badly" was ungrammatical and that we should say "feel bad." And we still complain about "feel badly."

I guess the point is that the language will grow and change or stay the same exactly as it pleases. And it's comforting to know that a century of assaults may have changed a word's meaning here or there, but it hasn't shaken the language's basic good sense one bit.

Speech is communication, too

Updating you on the rain event and trackage

When we think of writing, we think first of print, but writing is just as critical to the spoken words on television and radio. Radio listeners were reminded of this recently when a well-known sports writer and radio commentator used "creeped" instead of *crept* as a past tense for *creep*.

When professional wordsmiths fail to use words gracefully, or even correctly, the audience's esteem drops a bit. And the questions are the same whether for reader or listener: 1] How did this professional communicator make such a basic mistake in the first place, and 2] How did editors fail to catch it?

There's no shortage of linguistic disrepair in print, as any reader can testify. Nor are the electronic media exempt. The following is from just a bit of listening (I won't even *mention* the politician who said, "And this is just the tip of the *icebox*.")

■ Radio report from Santa Fe on the sale of Indian art:
  "Everybody is making money hand over foot." Hand over *fist*.
■ Radio. Discussion of a national institute for the environment:
  "Some questions and issues fall *between* the cracks."
  Whatever falls between the cracks doesn't fall very far. Fall *into* the cracks.

Updating you on the rain event

- A television anchor describes someone as "half English, half German and half Irish." An embarrassment of halves.
- Pronunciation of *recoup* from a radio reporter forever scarred by first-year French: "The agreement will allow them to *recoo* most of their investment."
- Television reporter describing an automobile accident: "The car vareened around the curve and went off the road." Vareened? Probably a hybrid of *careened* and *veered*.
- Television report on revamping Broadway's "Les Miserables" on its tenth anniversary: "However, *it begs the question*: How long is long enough?" The expression "begs the question" doesn't mean to provoke the question, or that the question begs to be asked. It means to use an argument that assumes as proved the very thing you're trying to prove.
- Television weather forecast: "This region can look forward to a *rain event*." What could a "rain event" be?
- Radio weather forecast: "The weather won't variate much to-day." *Vary*. "Variate" is probably a back formation of *variation*.
- Television news. "Police said they thought the incident was the work of vandalizers." *Vandal* is the noun. "Vandalizer" is probably created from the verb *vandalize*.
- Radio. Story on Koreans' adoration of their leaders: "There is not a store or shop or beauty parlor without a picture of *father and son hanging on the wall*." Quick, get the camera before Dad and Junior get off the wall.
- Radio traffic reporter. "There's an accident prior to the Inwood exit." *Prior to* means before in *time*, not location.
- Television. "The airplane *dove* from the sky." *Dived*.
- Radio. "Susan went as a personal visitor, but she *brought* along her tape recorder just in case." Back to the fourth grade! And while there, look up *bring* and *take*.

- Television. Story on transferring welfare responsibility to the states. "The governors know they're going to *take a hit* — they just want to be sure they're *at the table* when they take a hit." Are we dining or doing battle? Squash that mixaphor.

- Television commentator. "He rejects that theory and argues that the *causality runs the other way.*" Makes the listener want to run the other way, too.

- Radio. "Amtrak said that rail travel is safe, particularly where it owns all the trackage." Glad Hank Snow never got hold of that word "trackage": *See that big eight-wheeler comin' down the trackage, means your true-lovin' daddy ain't acomin' backage. He's movin' on. . . .*

- Radio. NATO jargon for pulling out of the Serb-Bosnian conflict: "*Self-extraction from a non-benign environment.*" One hears of people extracting themselves from difficult situations, but this is ridiculous.

- Television. A French diplomat on France's nuclear tests: "I don't like this word bomb. It is not a bomb. It is a device that explodes." Keep that up and pretty soon you'll be calling missiles "peacekeepers" the way we do.

- Television. We'll update you on the news from the business world when we come back. Update the news, not *me.*

- Radio. Political story. "Stay the course. . . the rule of the day. . . what he calls a new beginning. Reduce discrimination down to a level where class-action type action is not necessary — reduce it down to a level of insignificance." Speaking of reducing things to a "level of insignificance" — here, triteness is running to catch up with redundancy.

- Radio. "Roanoke, Va., is experiencing a significant drop in its crime rate." How would a city "experience" a drop?

Updating you on the rain event

Words such as *level, rate,* and *experience* often create wordy if not silly structures. When calling a catalog company recently to place an order, I heard this phone message: "We're sorry. We're experiencing unusual delays in responding to your call. Please stay on the line and. . . ." This common taped response is offensively silly. First, the tape was "experiencing" nothing. And even if it *could* experience something, it wouldn't be experiencing a delay. It was I who experienced the delay.

We all routinely hear such careless, illogical and imprecise communication, but readers and listeners alike hope for better from professional writers and editors.

column

22

Popular expressions

Misunderstanding is just a hair's breadth away

Previous columns have touched on misused and misunderstood words and expressions such as *begs the question* and *falling between the cracks.* Here are a few more.

Vocal cords are spelled that way. They have nothing to do with *chords.*

To the manner born. This expression is often incorrectly written "to the manor born." The words come from Shakespeare's Hamlet, who is discussing a certain custom of his homeland. Hamlet says he does not like the custom, though he is a "native here, and to the manner born." He means that he has grown up with the custom, not that he was born in a manor.

For all intents and purposes. Sometimes mistakenly rendered "for all *intensive* purposes."

A hair's breadth. The expression means by the narrowest margin — the width of a hair. Does the television news anchor who says someone escaped by "a hare's breath" ever wonder what that expression might mean?

Popular expressions

Chaise longue. The French words for "long chair" are not so much misunderstood as they are mispronounced and misspelled. The expression is pronounced *shez* (or *shaze*) long; it is neither pronounced nor spelled "chase lounge."

Forte, forte. One is French (correctly pronounced FORT), the other is Italian (pronounced fortAY), depending upon what we mean. If we're discussing someone's strong point, we want the French *forte* (FORT). If we're discussing a music direction meaning loud and forceful, we want the Italian *forte* (fortAY).

Even though these words and expressions are commonly misused, it's important for professional writers and editors to sidestep such problems. Many readers know a great deal about the language and will judge harshly those "wordsmiths" who seem to know less.

23 & 24

Zimmerman leads can put flesh on bare-bone facts

But dull is dull, despite device

Most journalists assume that human beings are more interesting than facts and figures and that, therefore, a "humanized" lead must be more interesting than a fact-and-figure lead. But that's true only if the people in the leads are indeed interesting.

Conversely, facts and figures are not necessarily bloodless. Neither are the ideas and issues they represent — if their effect on people is immediately clear.

The problem is that we seem to have only one method for humanizing leads. Someone coined an expression for that method — the Fred Zimmerman lead. It's a staple of the trade: We find one person who, in microcosm, represents everybody else, and we lead with that person.

When it works, it works fine.

But it often doesn't work. That's because we begin with some anonymous soul who does and says nothing very interesting. Oh, let's humanize this lead — we'll just stick this fellow Zimmerman at the top:

> *Fred Zimmerman takes down a box of cherry Jell-O from his shelf, reads the instructions and dumps the red powder into a bowl of boiling water.*

Last year Fred Zimmerman wouldn't have attempted that simple task — last year he couldn't read even such simple instructions.

"I know it doesn't sound like much, but I'm so grateful that now I can do these little things for myself," says Zimmerman.

As a functional illiterate, Zimmerman had lots of company. One in six adult males in Davis County can't read well enough to blah blah.

No, it certainly doesn't sound like much. If we can't find a Zimmerman more compelling than Fred, why don't we give up on this sort of lead and try something else? Why assume that *anybody* at all is more interesting than any idea? The word "humanize" doesn't mean simply to use something animate instead of inanimate; the word means to capture some human feeling, drama, or condition. Sometimes facts and figures capture that drama. And surely the fact that one in six males in the county can't read is more interesting than this unknown Fred and his ho-hum history with Jell-O.

Further, how would we tell this story if we were telling it? Face to face, we're natural story-tellers. And we'd never approach someone and say:

Boy oh boy, I just interviewed some man named Fred Zimmerman who made some Jell-O.

No. We'd say something like:

Imagine: One in six males in the county can't read and write well enough to take a driver's test or fill out a credit application or understand simple instructions. For example, I just spoke to a man who was all excited about being able to follow a recipe for making Jell-O!

If we were speaking, in other words, we'd know instinctively that we couldn't just launch into the Zimmerman anecdote — we'd need a set-up. But we seem to abandon our instincts when facing a blank computer screen. We forget that an approach that cannot work in person probably won't work in writing, either. An approach that works in person, however, can work well in writing — often with only slight changes.

Look at these two newspaper leads. (People and place names have been changed.)

1) The farms and woods where Harry Coleman grew up hunting deer and playing in Catfish Creek are disappearing. The school that Coleman attended in the '40s and '50s made way for Johnson's paper mill. The cotton gin managed by his father, Albert Coleman, is now Osbaugh's Market.

Catfish Creek Way was just a dirt road when Coleman and his family moved into a big white farmhouse there in the early '50s. Now, nearly 4,000 cars travel that road every day.

2) Hazel Wilson loves her new home in Willow Walk subdivision. The split-level house is decorated with blue paint and black trim and has a two-car garage, a porch in the back yard and a skylight in the bathroom. Wilson. . . moved to Willow Walk in May, and in doing so, has joined the migration to Jefferson County.

Say the truth: Do we really give one honest darn about Harry's old hunting grounds or Hazel's new house? We're surrounded by exciting stimuli in a sudden, complex and high-stakes world. Are we enchanted by these "humanized" leads? Then why kid ourselves that other readers will be? At the very least, we could compress those leads to capture the point as well as the Zimmerman:

1) Harry Coleman remembers when Catfish Creek Way was just a dirt road. Now, nearly 4,000 cars travel that road daily, and the Catfish Creek area is fast becoming a bustling bedroom community.

2) James and Hazel Wilson have joined the migration to western Jefferson County.

The point is that there's nothing inherently interesting or unusual about Harry or Hazel or their individual stories. Nothing says we can't use them to speed us to the heart of the story, but why dwell on them?

That doesn't mean, of course, that good Zimmermans don't exist. The leads below show us why the Zimmerman remains popular despite its many failures. Properly conceived and delivered, it's quick, interesting and hangs human flesh on bare-bone facts. The people in successful Zimmermans are more engaging than the facts — that's why they're there. They genuinely and interestingly represent the story, their comments are pertinent and succinct, and they can make potentially dry stories come alive.

Mitchell Zuckoff of *The Boston Globe* deals with pending child labor law that would conflict with certain provisions in the General Agreement on Tariffs and Trade:

Her name was Lesly Solorzano. And at 15, she was probably too young to be speaking for 200 million people.

But there she was, mustering her confidence and pushing back her soft black hair, telling members of the US Senate about the two years she spent making Liz Claiborne sweaters in a Honduran factory, working up to 80 hours a week for 38 cents an hour. . . .

She told them about the Korean factory managers who strike and belittle the young workers, and about the ones who 'like to touch the girls.' She told them about locked bathrooms, choking dust and impossible quotas.

Then she made what seemed to her a simple plea: Pass pending legislation, called the Child Labor Deterrence Act, that would outlaw US imports of all products made by children younger than 15.

But what neither she nor the estimated 200 million other child laborers worldwide could know was that, in the new age of global free trade, fulfilling her request would be anything but simple.

Merle English of *New York Newsday* puts a simple but intriguing little Zimmerman on a scam story: *Malkie B. thought she was making an investment. Instead, she lost her wedding and engagement rings and most of her family's life savings.*

Caleb Solomon of *The Wall Street Journal* uses one parent to get into this story about baby boomers who delayed having children and now find that parenthood "takes its toll on their stiff, creaking bodies."

To Wayne Grant, the 45-year-old dad of two blond, blue-eyed cherubs, life as father reminds him of the hazing and forced marches he endured more than a quarter of a century ago at West Point.

'You don't get much sleep, you have a lot of fatigue,' and, he adds, you get hurt. 'But I had an 18-year-old body then.'

Good Zimmermans often depend on a sense of drama as well as keen writing skill. Ken Armstrong of the *Chicago Tribune* writes about courts forcing parents to accompany their truant children to classes:

Jan Neely graduated from high school 21 years ago, but there she sits, in a classroom at Buffalo Grove High School, wishing she weren't there.

While the teenagers around her take spelling, math and social studies, Neely reads a book or does paperwork for a trucking company she recently started with her husband. Sometimes she steals away to the boiler room for a cigarette.

But if she leaves early, she goes to jail.

Mary Murphy of *The Orlando Sentinel* writes about the teen fad of drinking a flower tea that can cause hallucinations, fever, even death:

Jonathan Snyder couldn't breathe. The rattlesnakes coiled around his arms and slithered down his legs. . . .

The thrill-seeking 17-year-old got more than he expected from drinking tea brewed from the flowers of a common backyard plant: He ended up in a hospital.

The culprit was the lovely, delicate — and deadly — angel trumpet.

Inherently interesting and novel stories can be made even more so through the right Zimmerman. Jack Jackson, a contributing writer for *The Times Picayune*, begins his story about folks who work in the "cemetery business":

His friends call him the 'Roach Man.' He works among the dead, in an environment that would give many people the willies. He opens long sealed crypts and tombs, rearranges the mummified or decaying bodies inside, sweeps out deteriorating caskets (sometimes crawling way inside to do it), making room for the brand-new shiny casket that contains another body.

But Perry Mathieu, caretaker of St. Roch Cemeteries, says he has one of the best jobs in town.

These works show that strong Zimmermans — unlike the weak variety — are not tedious impediments that merely delay the story, but high-speed thoroughfares that speed straight to its heart.

25

Clause and effect

Backing in can wreck a lead

The opening words of a news story can either bring readers into the story or send them packing. That all-important beginning should not be crippled by graceless, fuzzy phrasing or by a formulaic, artificial structure that has little to do with conversational expression — let alone with clear communication.

Writers sometimes stuff the lead or limp into the story by backing in with some corollary bit of background rather than with the story's main point. An example:

Rejecting his 'lupus-induced mania' defense, a Tarrant County jury decided Wednesday that Robert Neville Jr. should die for the February abduction-slaying of Amy Robinson of Arlington.

To see how lame this beginning is, imagine saying to someone: "Rejecting his 'lupus-induced mania' defense. . . ." We wouldn't. We know instinctively that listeners need a subject — an actor to hang the action upon — and we don't want to confuse them with the first words out of our mouths. The "lupus-induced mania" defense should be dealt with later, when there's room to explain it.

The lead is fuzzy as well because "rejecting" refers to the following noun *jury*, and "his" refers to the following noun *Neville*. It's also weakened by dependence upon nouns rather than verbs *(the February abduction and slaying of)*. Nouns force us to add prepositions — notorious for creating wordy, dense sing-song.

A simple revision makes the lead clearer and more conversational:

"A Tarrant County jury, rejecting Robert Neville Jr.'s defense that disease caused his violence, sentenced him to death Wednesday for abducting and killing Amy Robinson of Arlington."

Here's a handful of backing-in clauses from a metropolitan newspaper. Each clause could be inserted immediately after the subject, or it could become a second sentence. (There's nothing wrong with leads of more than one sentence, and trying to keep them to one sentence accounts for many long and busy beginnings.)

"With a beaming group of Tuskegee Airmen looking on. . . ."

"As Danny Lee Barber was unexpectedly returned to his home on death row late Wednesday. . . ."

"On the 50th anniversary of the U. N. convention against genocide — adopted in the wake of the Holocaust — . . ."

"After being told of the 'enormous evil' of Chicago street gangs...."

Writers sometimes begin with a clause even when a tighter, more active approach is readily available:

In Lucinda Williams' best-known song, 'Passionate Kisses,' she sings about the simple pleasures she wants out of life — things such as a comfortable bed and a man to love and a really good place to rock out in.

'Is it too much to demand/To have a full house and a rock 'n' roll band?'

Backing in is hardly the only problem here. First, that snippet of song should be cut. It gets in the way because it says something different from the lead and therefore fails to reinforce, amplify or verify the lead.

Logic suffers, too: A comfortable bed and someone to love might be called simple or universal pleasures, but a "full house and a rock 'n' roll band" are neither simple nor universal — they're complex and specific to the singer. (And many would not even consider them "pleasures.")

A man to love is not a "thing." And a "*really* good place" should be recast. Vague qualifiers such as *really, somewhat, quite, rather, extremely, basically, totally* and *completely* don't help us write precisely. Skip such qualifiers if they merely magnify or reduce the imprecise word that follows. Instead, find the precise word. Revision:

"Lucinda Williams names her pleasures in her best-known song, 'Passionate Kisses' — a comfortable bed, someone to love and somewhere to rock 'n' roll."

Backing in can often create dangling modifiers: *While walking downtown, the trees were in bloom.* The practice doesn't have to involve the lead to cause such problems:

A colorful character, Mr. Hunt's celebrity linked Dallas to oil in much the same way that Microsoft Corp.'s Bill Gates has tied Seattle to technology.

Hunt's celebrity is a colorful character?

Wordiness and awkward phrasing also damage this passage: "linked Dallas to oil in much the same way that" (*that* should be *as*). Consider, as well, "Microsoft Corp.'s Bill Gates." That cumbersome ID is goody-two-shoes writing — particularly when dealing with someone as well known as Bill Gates — and it destroys the passage's energy and pace. Remember that newspaper readers are not stupid, and save the dispensable for later. Better:

"The celebrated Mr. Hunt linked Dallas to oil much as Bill Gates tied Seattle to technology."

Backing in can present yet another problem when the clause is followed by attribution rather than by a subject. Writers often forget that buried attribution is an insertion and must be set off with a *pair* of commas. Omitting the comma after the attribution distorts meaning. Examples:

"After misstating the delegate's intent, he said the translators were dismissed." This sentence says he made his statement *after* he misstated the delegate's intent.

"In a 1986 memorandum, she said Smith wrote that the meeting with that group never took place." This says she made her statement in a 1986 memo.

"Because the bill may be inconsistent with religious freedom, he said there's still a chance it could be blocked." This means that he made his statement *because* the bill may be inconsistent with religious freedom.

A good lead will draw readers into the story if it is direct, conversational and interesting. And once into the story, the readers should find the work precise, graceful and grammatical as well.

Avoiding the predictable

When the drop-dead lead is just a dead lead

Media writers work hard on their all-important leads. They know that if they don't grab the readers right away, they may lose the chance.

Sometimes that hard work pays off in fresh, clear, bright beginnings. And sometimes it doesn't. Too often the search for a catchy lead results in a hackneyed gimmick or journalistic cliché. This column might have begun, for example, with a "dictionary lead": *Webster's defines 'hackneyed' as 'to make common or frequent use of.'*

The dictionary lead is among the threadbare approaches that appear regularly in the news media although such leads fail to engage and are sometimes even ridiculous. Here's an impromptu collection of such beginnings, nearly all of them actual leads culled from newspapers across the country.

Seasonal silliness, calendar clichés and almanac mania leads. This approach ties the story to something — a holiday, an anniversary, or an event — whether or not that something has anything to do with the story:

■ *Yesterday was April Fool's Day, but it was no joke when Dottie Varnes' new BMW was stolen from the Jefferson St. parking ramp.*

Drop-dead lead

- *Ninety-two years ago this month, the Wright brothers broke the bonds of gravity. And Lynyrd Skynyrd's Sunday night performance soared to new heights as well.*
- *The Arlington City Council is ringing in the New Year with three new proposals for dealing with the city's gang problems.*

One-word leads. The tiresomeness of the one-word start is generally exceeded only by its clumsiness:

- *Learn.*
  That's what emergency planners plan to do in the wake of their brush with Hurricane Felix.

Duh leads. The *duh* approach is flawed because it tells us what we already know. Worse, it often attributes the non-information. Readers respond to leads like the one below: We need a study to tell us this?

- *As the country approaches the 1996 elections, many Americans are deeply troubled over the course of the nation, particularly its economic health and the state of families, according to a new study.*

List leads. The problem with the list beginning is that a list is all it is. It makes a poor start because, without a context, it says nothing:

- *Flowers. Stuffed bears. Slowly turning pinwheels. A child-sized basketball. All are signs of joy and playfulness.*

- *Final exams. Athletic events. College admission. A relative's illness. Emotional release. The reasons teenagers pray reflect the shape of their lives.*

"Things like this aren't supposed to happen" leads. The language, as well as the assumption, damns these leads. Who *is* "supposed" to get cancer, drown on vacation, be abducted, murdered, raped, abused? And quoting ridiculous words doesn't make them any less ridiculous.

- *Burdette Johnson wasn't supposed to get cancer.*
- *It was to have been a holiday; longtime friends spending a week together at the beach before getting back to the real world. Instead, the real world has run them over. 'Things like this aren't supposed to happen to people you know,' said Michelle McCammon, 21.*

"It didn't used to be this way" leads. What can we say — things change. And maybe the good old days had their problems, too.

- *Mary Staton, 63, remembers more peaceful, caring times in Portsmouth, when neighbors trusted and looked out for each other and children played together safely on the streets.*
- *A decade ago, the Riddick family was full of hope, dreams and plans for the future.*

Fooled you, fooled you leads. These are dirty-trick beginnings, promising but not delivering:

- *Decapitated missionaries. A deranged man jumping from a 15th-floor window. The sex act in progress. Those are pictures you'll never see in most newspapers.*
- *The scene at Fairfax Airport was one of carnage — bodies strewn over the tarmac, the air filled with the cries of the wounded and dying. Emergency crews set up crisis facilities and worked quickly to help wherever they could.*

  But none of it was real. It was the city's first drill to see how the city would react in a large-scale emergency such as a plane crash.

The answer is no leads. Question leads are often frowned upon, but they can work well if carefully handled. Among the questions to avoid are those that evoke a "no," a "who cares?" or a "beats the hell outta me":

■ *Want to be a midwife?*

■ *Ever wonder how Fortune 500 company execs start their day?*

■ *How many times do you suppose Wilfred Rob Willis has remembered the crazy '60s?*

This beginning by Neil Strauss of *The New York Times*, however, redeems the question lead:

■ *How many people have you killed in your lifetime? Have you shot them with a cap gun or a cocked forefinger in a game of cops and robbers? Have you blown them up with a laser or torn their heads off in a video game?*

Simulated murder has become an accepted form of play in American culture. Such games are the only way we're allowed to live out our destructive impulses without crossing moral or legal boundaries.

Strauss' lead shows us that in certain hands, everything works — even devices that in uncertain hands have become threadbare.

column

27

The light approach

In writing, humor is serious business

You can't talk about freshness in media writing without also talking about humor or a sense of play.

Humor, a natural part of our world, should be a natural part of media writing, too. Instead, it's rare. Or it doesn't work. Not all writers are outfitted for fun, it seems, and we cringe at strained humor, lame word play, or flat jokes.

Much fresh, playful, or humorous writing depends upon our collective experience of pop culture. From *The Wall Street Journal's* John J. Keller: *Ma Bell has fallen down. Can new leadership help her get up?*

Keller's lead amuses us because it plays on a television ad that also — perversely, perhaps — amused us. It also shows that a light approach to a serious story about big business can be appropriate — although a light approach to a serious story about an *individual* probably would not be. Such leads must work even for readers who don't get the joke, and this one does. Keller's words would be meaningful even to those unfamiliar with the TV ad.

Richard Sine of *The Philadelphia Inquirer* also uses shared experience for the following clever lead. (The parentheses in the second paragraph are Sine's.)

In a statement against student shortcuts, Villanova University administrators plan to stop selling Cliffs Notes at the school bookstore, drawing praise from faculty and barbs from student leaders and the guides' publishers.

(The foregoing was a brief synopsis of this story. Continue reading to learn the details and nuances, or you can stop right here and pretend you read the whole thing.)

With that lead, Sine manages to poke gentle fun not only at an academic icon, but at the journalistic icon of the summary lead as well. And again, he provides enough information for all readers to enjoy the lead, including those who may not know what Cliffs Notes are.

Look at the following fresh lead by Julia Prodis, a fine writer for The Associated Press:

Like a doctor feeling for a pulse, Dave Honaker lays his hands on the wide, plastic hose. It begins to vibrate as pebbles and dirt rush through. It shudders a bit, then is still.

Honaker smiles. The furry body of a prairie dog, still in its subterranean hole, is plugging the end of the hose. It's only a matter of time now.

'You can feel when he's fighting back,' Honaker yells over the roar of the powerful suction. 'He's got a good hold, and then he loses it.'

Just then, the hose jolts, and with a rumbling whoosh, the rodent shoots up the hose. 'One!' Honaker mouths, his eyes gleaming with excitement.

A moment later, another whoosh. 'Two!'

'It's like playing the violin,' Honaker says modestly. 'After five years, you get a little better.' Honaker is a master of the latest in rodent-control technology — the prairie dog vacuum.

Julia begins with a descriptive scene-setter that does what a scene-setter is supposed to do, but often does not — provoke curiosity. She also (in a passage not seen here) addresses reader concern for the prairie dogs early in the story by writing that the animals are not hurt, just relocated. A light touch is always appropriate for win/win stories — here, a goofy contraption lets landowners stop poisoning prairie dogs and yet be rid of them.

Michelle Boorstein, another AP writer, adds both humor and voice to this lead with the words "sounds more like a politician than a saboteur":

A letter left at the scene of the Amtrak derailment rages at abuses by federal police agencies, then ends with a demand that sounds more like a politician than a saboteur: 'It is time for an independent federal agency to police the law enforcement agencies and other government employees.'

Humor in newswriting must be handled with care because it often displays the writer's voice. (By "voice" in this context, I mean *presence* rather than opinion.) In certain kinds of important or sensitive "just the facts, ma'am" stories, the writer's voice, no matter how pleasing, can be seen as inappropriate, intrusive, and unwelcome.

One *hopes* for voice from columnists, however. Blackie Sherrod, a *Dallas Morning News* columnist, has a savvy command of the language, a nicely developed sense of humor, and great voice. He often exercises all three to make valid and interesting points:

Just the other day, during a respite from translating Aristotle, I gazed at the horizon and wondered vaguely whatever happened to Deanna Durbin. Immediately, a sizable portion of the populace sprang to its feet and said as follows:

Who?

This is perhaps the cruelest response a 'celebrity' could hear. To most persons who blossom in limelight, recognition is as vital as beans, if not oxygen. Especially denizens in the entertainment dodge, film, theater and sports. If you failed to give Don King a second look of recognition, he would disintegrate, a prospect that makes your little heart pound.

These leads suggest that fresh approaches and formulaic approaches are mutually exclusive. They also suggest that only the fresh approach is fun — for reader *and* writer.

28

Fresh approaches

The right detail can make you want more

In a world of fads, journalism is no exception. The development *du jour*, whether in content or presentation, can sweep through the industry in months.

It happens in writing, too. Where we have one-minute managers, we also have one-minute writing coaches. Inverted pyramids are in, then out. Suddenly summary leads are scorned, and the narrative is trumpeted as though it's something *new*. Anecdotes tell the story best; no, they don't. Humanize everything because facts and figures are boring. They are? To whom?

The fact is that none of this stuff is any more in than it's out. Good writing — writing that engages, enlightens and entertains — is always in. And writing that bores and bewilders is always out. Writing is both harder and easier than using gimmicks — harder if we think gimmicks will make us good, and easier if we forget gimmicks and use instead the stuff of our creative intellects. (We'll look at some journalistic gimmicks later in this series.)

Briefly — and fads aside — in the hands of gifted writers, everything works, and in the hands of poor writers, almost nothing does.

That doesn't mean we can't learn more about good writing by analyzing it. Good writers are always observing, always teaching themselves. If we don't exactly have a *gift*, we can still practice a fine *craft*. Most of the good writing in the media is craft, anyway. It's not that art can't and doesn't happen in media writing — it's that, as readers, editors and writers, we can't expect, demand or promise it. But we *can* expect, demand and promise a solid and responsible craft.

That said, let's examine the *device* in the fresh approaches of some fine writers. We'll assume at the outset that good *reporting* forms the foundation of good newswriting. Dazzling writing without solid reporting yields only flash without light, form without content.

Good reporting gathers that invaluable detail. For example, newspapers carried many moving leads when the Oklahoma bombing survivors and families testified in the McVeigh trial — but none more moving than this lead from Rick Bragg of *The New York Times*. With a few telling details, Rick captures the awful and personal meaning of the blast.

After the explosion, people learned to write left-handed, to tie just one shoe. They learned to endure the pieces of metal and glass embedded in their flesh, to smile with faces that made them want to cry, to cry with glass eyes. They learned, in homes where children had played, to stand the quiet. They learned to sleep with pills, to sleep alone.

Today, with the conviction of Timothy J. McVeigh. . . .

From Associated Press writer Charles J. Hanley comes a great lead made greater by the stuff of good reporting — the right details.

He's out there somewhere in the wild gorges of the Yuat River, hunting pig, harvesting yam, a young tribesman whose heart belongs to the jungle — but whose blood belongs to the U.S. government.

Or so says Patent No. 5,397,696.

113

Yes, you want more — that's the whole idea. Suffice it to say that Charles Hanley's story is about "genetic colonialism," and that the United States has patented the blood cells of one of the planet's most primitive citizens. The dry and bloodless detail of the patent number, paired as it is with the idea of real blood, is also dry with an intelligent irony that promotes interest and curiosity.

Sometimes writers can use one detail as a symbol or artifact that will in turn lead to the heart of the story. NYT writer Michael Specter uses such a device in this Grozny story by first focusing on the road leading the refugees to safety.

There is only one open road left into this city. It is a long series of bomb craters, really, mixed with dirt, mud and occasionally some asphalt. The road starts in the deep woods just southwest of town and runs straight toward the ravaged center.

The road has no name, but it does not need one, because everybody knows what it is there for. It is the last, harrowing route to safety each day for thousands of anguished refugees who have been driven from their homes here in the capital of Chechnya. . . and it is the best entry route for the secessionist rebels who now reign over most of the city.

Choosing a detail that approaches the subject obliquely through an unexpected but certainly not unrelated set of eyes can bring a fresh point of view to a story. Ellen Warren and Cathleen Falsani of the *Chicago Tribune* used this approach when Cardinal Joseph Bernardin died. Their lead captures the beloved figure's impact not by focusing on Cardinal Bernardin himself, but by focusing instead on a child's perspective.

The children arriving at Blessed Sacrament School in North Lawndale, giggling and goofing around, knew immediately that some-thing important had happened.

114

Fresh approaches

Bundled lumps of mittened energy watching their breath turn to fog, the youngsters entered the main hallway Thursday morning, but all was dark. And quiet as a church.

Clutching Daddy's hand, they wondered in big, audible whispers — what was going on?

The only light was the unreliable flicker of a single red candle on a table in the hall, and soon the children knew. . . . On the table with the candle, they spotted a framed photograph of Cardinal Joseph Bernardin.

Those offerings suggest that the right detail is invaluable to fresh writing — and also that there are as many original approaches as there are original writers.

29

Allusions

Food for the mind, nourishment for the soul

James Stewart gets soused in the 1940 movie "The Philadelphia Story," and Cary Grant, while gamely fixing him yet another drink, mumbles something about "carrying coals to Newcastle." The allusion enriches and amuses: England's Newcastle is a famous coal center — it needs coal the way Stewart's character needs another drink.

Because allusions are the province of the well-read, or at least the educated, we're sometimes reluctant to use them. We fear readers won't understand. But allusions are rich devices for adding color and depth to our communication, and their loss contributes to the general flatness of much writing. After all, making connections is the business of the active mind, and the allusion is both a result and a *cause* of connection. "The *yin* and the *yang* of the sports world," says a CNN newscaster, and in two words connects with readers around the world who know he means *two opposites that make up the whole.*

We need avoid only two kinds of allusions: the rarely used and the overused. The rarely used are obscure and may bewilder; the overused are nothing more than clichés. (Two examples of currently overused allusions are *bully pulpit* and *fin de siècle*.)

Allusions

Beyond that, to be on the planet is to collect allusions. Oh, there's *trouble in River City*, we say, or *something rotten in the state of Denmark*. I'm a *Type A*; you're a *Svengali*; she's a *Lazarus*; he's a *Pygmalian*. Whoever, we're all just *hoi polloi* suffering *Sturm und Drang* and will end up in the *slough of despond* unless our *Waterloo* also turns out to be a *road to Damascus*. *Sisypheans* all, we push big rocks up long hills. We nurse *Achilles' heels*, fret under the *sword of Damocles* and are *hoist on our own petard*. We suspect *Trojan Horses* and clean *Augean stables*. We allude to *Armageddon*, the *Holocaust* and *Gotterdammerung*.

Sometimes we're so good at allusions that we combine them with word play — as we see in this example from a sale sign in a sporting goods store. It alluded to Shakespeare's "Now is the winter of our discontent":

> Now is the discount
>
> On our winter tents

We use literature in just such interesting ways to emphasize our messages. The effective allusion works on all levels: Those who don't "get it" are none the worse because they don't know there's anything to "get." And those who *do* get it share a bit of subterranean pleasure with the writer or speaker. Our understanding of Faulkner's title, *The Sound and the Fury*, is deepened if we know that he took it from the Shakespearean tragedy *MacBeth*. The words come from MacBeth's soliloquy near the play's end. There, he says that life is a tale told by an idiot, full of sound and fury, signifying nothing. The message is nihilistic, and one supposes Faulkner chose it for the light it could cast on his novel's meaning as well as because his narrator was "backward" — thus, a tale told by an "idiot."

Aldous Huxley's title, *Brave New World*, also comes from Shakespeare. The words are from *The Tempest* — in which the innocent Miranda cries: "O brave new world/that has such people in 't." The words in Miranda's mouth are hopeful and genuine, but Huxley's work is a satire. His title registers with every reader as ironic, but it's *doubly* ironic for readers who know its origin. Likewise, Hemingway's title *For Whom the Bell Tolls* is more meaningful if we know he got it from John Donne and that Donne's passage continues: It tolls for *thee*.

Allusions to Babbitt or babbitry are frequent enough that we understand by context that those words mean a smug middle-class conformity. But, again, the allusion means more if we know it comes from Sinclair Lewis' scathing 1922 novel, titled for its materialistic and self-satisfied main character.

The expressions "the center cannot hold" or "slouching toward Bethlehem" are intensified if we've read poet William Butler Yeats' "Second Coming." Then, when a financial columnist writes, for example, that "Wall Street is acting as though the center will not hold," the statement has special impact. After the re-issue of "The Manchurian Candidate," a movie reviewer put a special twist on "slouching towards Bethlehem" when he wrote that the movie goes *grinning towards Bethlehem*. And Peter DeVries made an "in" joke as well when he titled one of his comic novels *Slouching Towards Kalamazoo*.

Whenever someone alludes to the "remembrance of things past," we recall Marcel Proust. When we hear the word "quixotic" or the expression "tilting at windmills," we remember Don Quixote, and we know why those terms mean well-intentioned but futile. When someone mentions a Faustian bargain, we know we're talking about selling our souls to the devil — because that's what Goethe's Faust did. "The last hurrah" is a rich and meaningful term made more so if we know Edwin O'Connor's study of a politician's life. George Orwell's *1984* gave us "Big Brother," a term meaning a deceitful and obtrusive government. And our word "doublespeak" is a hybrid of Orwell's "newspeak" and "doublethink." Voltaire's *Candide* gave us the popular expression "the best of all possible worlds." We took "no man is an island" from John Donne and "fearful symmetry" from William Blake.

The richness that allusion brings belongs in the communication of the literate. Sure, we can get by — writer and reader alike — without knowing the origin and significance of these and myriad other rich allusions. We all can take pleasure in a sale sign that reads: "Now is the discount on our winter tents" — whether or not we know Shakespeare. But intimacy with the sources of such expression blesses us twice: when we first come to know them and, forever after, when we meet them again.

Important imports

Some common foreign expressions have no English equivalent

Media writers sometimes fret over whether to use certain foreign words or expressions. *Has the term been sufficiently absorbed into English? Should I define it or let it stand alone?*

No single guideline covers all circumstances. Whether we should use a foreign term — with or without a definition — depends not only upon the term itself, but also upon what we're writing and our audience and intent.

Some foreign words are so firmly entrenched in the language that we needn't wonder whether we should use them — of course we should. Examples that leap to mind are *genre, angst, modus operandi, noblesse oblige, wunderkind, bon mot, film noir, nouveau riche, élan, idiot savant, chutzpah, bon mot, du jour.* . . . The list goes on. Such words are the domain of the literate.

The demand for clarity and simplicity does not rule out the use of common foreign words as long as we use them judiciously and accurately — and as long as they are the best words for the context. In all cases, however, writers' vocabularies should be *their* vocabularies — natural and unstrained. Intimacy with any word involves seeing that word in action over time and in different contexts. We don't get that intimacy with a visit to a foreign dictionary, or by knowing only a term's literal translation.

Literal translation may not mirror the word's original meaning. *Bon mot* literally means "good word," for example, but that hardly captures the expression's essence — a witty remark. The literal translation of *fin de siècle* is "end of century," but that interpretation loses the original's sense of decadence and weariness. *Bête noire* means "black beast," but that translation fails to conjure the meaning of *the* monster, singular and chief.

Generally, when a foreign term has an *exact* equivalent in English, we should use English. The exact equivalent of *de facto*, for example, is *in fact* — and that's a quicker, clearer term for an English-speaking audience. Likewise, why use *raison d'être* — however well known it may be — when its English twin, "reason for being," means the same thing and is immediately clearer? And in media writing, the Latin abbreviations *i.e.* (id est) and *e.g.* (exempli gratia) are more sensibly rendered "that is" and "for example."

Some valuable foreign words and expressions don't have English equivalents, though. In such instances, we would use the foreign terms because we have no other. And we would define them or not depending upon context and how widely understood the terms are.

Here are some tricky foreign terms often seen in print and that are useful for both writer and reader to know. We see them often in print not only because they are rich in meaning but because we have no exact English equivalent.

Gemütlichkeit (guh-MOOT-luh-kite): a feeling of warm, comfortable and homey cordiality.

Sang-froid (sahng-FWAH): Literally, "cold blood." The expression means to remain cool, calm and poised in unsettling or unsafe circumstances.

Gestalt (guh-SHTALT): a configuration or entity in which the whole is more than the sum of its parts.

Sine qua non (see-neh-kwah-NOHN): Literally, "without which not." The expression identifies the ingredient or condition without which something could not be; a prerequisite.

Schadenfreude (SHAH-den-FROY-duh) means to take a malicious pleasure in the misfortunes of others.

Lebensraum (LAY-benz-ROWM) is a good example of a word that is appropriate only in certain contexts. Although its literal meaning is "living space," it would be odd to find it in, say, an interior decorating article. The word is freighted with special meaning because it was Nazi Germany's excuse for invading and seizing territory. We usually see the word in the context of that history and association.

Leitmotiv (LIGHT-moh-TEEF), which means "leading motive," is appropriate in a classical music or literary context, but might be better expressed elsewhere as a "recurring theme." This word, too, has meaning beyond its literal translation — in this case, through its association with Richard Wagner's idea that repeating a theme or idea strengthens its dramatic impact.

Cognoscenti (koh-nyo-SHEN-tee): This Italian word means "experts," but that literal definition hardly captures the word's (often ironic) sense of having superior information, of being on the inside or in the know.

Sturm und Drang (SHTURM oont DRAHNG), which means "storm and struggle," is widely used to refer to anything excessively emotional or to turmoil or upheaval in general. The term derives from an 18th century romantic literary movement in Germany known for drama, passion, individualism and nationalism.

Zeitgeist (TSITE-geyst; the second syllable rhymes with "heist"): the spirit of a particular time.

Important imports

Again, the question of whether to use a foreign term depends on a variety of considerations, but when appropriate, such terms can enrich and deepen our work. The main thing is to use them naturally and accurately. As always, the more we know about language — and the more thoughtful we are about it — the better able we are to serve our audience.

The one reason *not* to use foreign — or any — language is to show off. Clear and precise writers use language to communicate, never to impress.

Making the difficult easy
Analogies can help readers understand

A constant journalistic challenge is that of presenting difficult or unfamiliar stories in a simple, accurate, clear and interesting way. Certain stories are inherently forbidding — technical and specialized stories involving economics, business, law or science come to mind. Such stories encourage — often seem to *demand* — density and detail that many readers find off-putting.

Clarity and a conversational style are necessary to making difficult stories easy to read. With those attributes in place, though, the analogy often can clear a difficult story's rough patches. Because analogies relate the unfamiliar to the familiar, they put flesh on otherwise dry bones. They make connections, put difficult notions or numbers in perspective and even create pictures.

Here are two analogies from *Dallas Morning News* writer Bruce Tomaso. Bruce is trying in the first passage to help the reader understand and perhaps visualize an acre-foot of water. In the second, he's dealing with 52 million acre-feet of water. In either story, he's not satisfied with simply defining an acre-foot — that is, offering the reader a meaningless number. And he localizes the second analogy to make it even more suggestive to *Dallas Morning News* readers.

Making the difficult easy

1) *Mesa's rural acreage includes the rights to 30,000 acre-feet of water. An acre-foot is 325,851 gallons, roughly enough to sustain a family of four for one year.*

2) *About 52 million acre-feet of water will remain under irrigable land in the High Plains by the year 2030. An acre-foot, the equivalent of 325,851 gallons, is the amount of water needed to cover an acre to a depth of one foot. Fifty-two million acre-feet, spread over Dallas, would submerge everything less than 20 stories tall.*

Sometimes journalists get the best analogies from their sources. Here, a professor of economics shows one way to clarify and make concrete the abstract business of the national debt:

If we increase taxes for only those people in the labor force (about 120 million people), balancing the federal budget will require a tax increase of more than $3,300 per working person per year. That's not a one-time increase, but an annual increase.

Moreover, this will not reduce the outstanding debt of the U.S. government, which is currently about $4 trillion (or $4 million million); such a tax increase will simply stop our nation's debt from increasing any further.

Scott Burns, a financial columnist for *The Dallas Morning News*, tackles the problem of describing the federal deficit with this fresh and imaginative analogy:

How rich is Ross Perot? You can get some idea of how large $3.3 billion is by measuring it against mutual funds and corporations.

■ *If Perot held 100 percent of his assets in one fixed-income fund, it would rank number 19 of the 1,140 fixed-income funds followed by Morningstar.*

- *If he held all his money in a stock fund, it would rank 23rd of 1,214 funds. Alternatively, he could own about a sixth of the $19. 7 billion Magellan Fund. . . .*
- *If Ross Perot were a corporation, he would be worth more than Knight Ridder Inc., Genentech, Reebok International, or Texas Instruments.*

Again, you might measure Perot's wealth against that of the average family — about $45,000. By that measure, he has the wealth of about 73,000 families, which is about the same as a city the size of Peoria, Ill.

Perot has three checking accounts; the largest paid him a million dollars in interest last year.

Is there any way that Ross Perot's wealth doesn't appear enormous? Yes.

At the current rate, Perot could cover the federal deficit for three days.

After that, he would be penniless.

Tom Siegfried, *Dallas Morning News* science editor, often uses analogy to help readers into his difficult subjects:

Imagine that a mysterious animal enters your front door every day at noon. By 1 p.m. it has found its way to the kitchen, and you observe that it is either a dog or a cat.

After some experimenting, you find that if you put out cat food in the morning, a cat will show up later; if you use dog food, the animal will be a dog. So far, no problem.

But suppose you wait until 12:30 to put out the food — after the animal has entered, but before you have seen it. At 1 p.m. you will still find a cat if you used cat food, a dog if dog food, even though the choice was made after the animal had come into the house.

Making the difficult easy

It seems absurd, but it's exactly what happens in the bizarre world of subatomic physics.

A story needn't be technical, however, to benefit from a well-presented analogy — making connections can give perspective to any work. Mary Williams Walsh of the *Los Angeles Times* helps American readers understand a hate crime story from Germany by drawing likenesses to the O.J. Simpson trial. The four men accused of firebombing a Turkish family's house and killing and injuring eight women and children were found guilty in this case, however:

The much-watched trial had been called Germany's counterpart to the O.J. Simpson proceedings, as it included questions of racism and possible police misconduct. The five-judge panel found itself, as did the Simpson jury, called upon to right social wrongs that had little direct bearing on the actual facts of the case.

And, as with the Simpson trial, after the verdicts were read, some Germans remained uncertain that justice really had been served.

Short analogies are welcome, too. From David Stipp of *The Wall Street Journal*:

These are, to be exact, spotted salamanders. Black, six inches long and spotted with bright yellow polka dots, they resemble baby alligators in overtight clown suits.

Paul Blythe of the *Palm Beach Post*:

If accounts of some diseases read like horror stories, then Guillain-Barre syndrome is a disease for the theater of the absurd.

Making the difficult easy

William Grimes, *The New York Times Magazine*:

It's a quiet site. You can hear the gentle sizzling of high-tension wires from the electrical substation serving the construction works.
Hundreds of precast concrete tunnel segments lie baking in the sun — Snack Chips of the Gods.

Whether long or short, the careful analogy is a gift to the reader because it brings depth and clarity to our writing.

32

Literary tricks

Don't be afraid to write stories that read like fiction

This column frequently deals with clarity and simplicity in writing, and often those qualities alone are enough to make writing sparkle. Once the underpinnings of clarity are in place, however, word play and literary techniques can help make ordinary work extraordinary.

Linguistic devices such as simile, metaphor and analogy have a place in certain kinds of media writing, and so do fiction-writing techniques such as foreshadowing or symbolism. The trick is knowing when and how much.

The word "fiction" often frightens people who deal in fact, but it needn't. Many of the devices that work well in fictional story-telling also work well in factual story-telling. Content rather than mechanic is the critical thing: One story may be actual and the other created, but both are more (or less) interesting because of how they're told.

Skillful writers excel at original, evocative and appropriate figurative language because it can add color, energy and depth to their work. That word *original* is important. There's no shortage of metaphor. But just grabbing what's there rather than creating fresh images will yield flat and hackneyed work. The best writers are never trite, in part because they do their own work.

Good figurative images needn't be — probably shouldn't be — intricate or curious. They need only be natural and visual and right. The simile is one of the simplest figures of speech, but still has great image-making power. It's a quick-take contrivance that can make features and profiles spring to life. A simile likens one thing to another and uses such words as *like* or *as*. Dorothy Parker gave us, for example, a woman whose "voice was as intimate as the rustle of sheets." D. H. Lawrence created a man whose "back was tense as a tiger's."

But you don't have to be a novelist to employ similes. Blackie Sherrod, a *Dallas Morning News* sports columnist, is a skillful creator of such figures of speech. One of Blackie's subjects is "as supple as a buggy whip." Another is "as colorful as a dump truck."

Similes can be dispensed economically to enliven a passage. "The show runs like a new Mercedes," writes one reporter. A music critic writes: "Bach's vaulting, cathedral-like score was reduced to a picky, pale semblance of itself, with notes ticked off like numbers on a speedometer."

Clint Williams of *The Arizona Republic* begins this lead with a simile: "Like a mooching second cousin from out of town, 100 degrees arrived in Phoenix on June 10 and would not leave." Ron Wolfe of the *Arkansas Democrat Gazette* ends a descriptive passage with a simile that successfully describes how the stomach feels around a loud noise: "Cannons shake the ground. A half-pound of black powder touched off in one blast — it knocks loose a fall of green leaves all around, and the sound lands in the pit of the stomach like having swallowed a rock." And Philip Martin, also of the *Arkansas Democrat Gazette*, lets similes deepen the meaning of this descriptive passage: "They were still there, of course, in sooty gray-black or blued or nickeled or plated with stainless steel, each a variation on the Ideal Pistol, the mythic American equalizer. Under the rapid flutter of fluorescent light, they glinted like so much cold and precious jewelry, latent and safe as snakes behind museum glass."

Be careful not to overdo. As we saw from these examples, a sprinkle of word play is suggestive. But a deluge brings garble. This quote from a one-time member of the Baltimore City Council shows what happens when figurative language runs amok: "[This] is a little snowball that rolled down the hill, that gathered moss, and when it got to the bottom, became a big mushroom."

Such speakers are great to quote, but not to emulate.

We also should remember that effective figurative language is appropriate. There's no reason to trick out sow's ear news stories with silk purse gimmicks. Nobody wants the school board meeting story to proceed: *School superintendent Joan Dean's back was as tense as a tiger's when angry parents, chins jutting out like dreadnoughts bearing down on a U-boat, confronted her on the district's new dress code. Superintendent Dean's eyes, lost in the fatty ridges of her face, looked like two pieces of coal pressed into a lump of dough.*

That last simile is from William Faulkner. Oh, well. As we said, the trick is knowing when and how much, and even gifted writers can overdo.

33

Sound and sense

If not overdone, poetic devices can enrich your writing

If Shakespeare wrote for public broadcasting or CNN, he'd be as famous for his sound bites as for his iambic pentameter. The Bard knew how to write to please the ear — something media writers give little if any thought. But even words read silently echo in the reader's head, so how they sound is crucial to polished work.

Some journalists consider literary or poetic devices the province of that master of purple prose, Edward Bulwer-Lytton. Others consider them inappropriate to the journalistic demands of clarity, brevity and objectivity. But fresh and memorable phrasing can only enhance those qualities.

In any event, the best media writers regularly use literary or poetic devices — by instinct if not intent.

Finding the sound that echoes the sense can bring us closer to ear-pleasing writing. We want the right word not only in meaning, but also in sound, suggestion, rhythm and tone. One way writers find sounds that echo the sense is through onomatopoeia — words that sound like what they mean (for example, *hiss, buzz, tinkle*). The following passage, by sports columnist David Casstevens of *The Arizona Republic*, is onomatopoeic:

Another trainer was busily at work, taping Hatcher's paws. There was the shriek of the adhesive, drawn in bursts off its spool, the flurry of Hatcher's fists as he spun the tape around them.

Look at the soft, hissing sounds in that passage. They reinforce meaning by imitating the sound of the tape whisking from the spool.

Aside from onomatopoeia, this passage is also notable for sibilance, which comes from consonants that hiss: S, Z, Sh, Ch, J. Sibilance brings a shushing, whispering sound to a passage and is both pleasing and highly suggestive. The sounds of the sea, for example, are usually termed *sibilant*.

Other devices that help make pleasing sounds are alliteration, consonance, assonance and resonance. Each creates certain effects — and each can be ludicrous if overdone.

Alliteration is the repetition of an initial sound, usually a beginning consonant or cluster — for example: *part and parcel, bag and baggage, stem to stern*. It's a simple and common linguistic device, yet it often creates striking or memorable prose. I used alliteration when I wrote: "Some journalists consider literary or poetic devices the province of that master of purple prose, Edward Bulwer-Lytton." *Poetic, province* and *purple prose* alliterate. (My rough draft read the "province of that prince of purple prose," which seemed one alliteration too many, so I changed *prince* to *master*.)

Dallas Morning News sports columnist Blackie Sherrod uses alliteration to good effect in this fragment: "his stubby fingers still flailing like a furious turtle."

Consonance, a word meaning harmony, also relates to sound. It's a repetition of consonants occurring anywhere in a word (*stick/stuck, march/lurch*). Blackie Sherrod again: "His chin juts out like a dreadnought bearing down on a U-boat." Read that sentence aloud to hear the high energy that results from the repetition of the

T sound. (And never mind that in *real* war, dreadnoughts don't spar with U-boats. The imagery is figurative.)

Assonance results when stressed vowel sounds are alike — often in internal rhyme. Brad Bailey, formerly a *Dallas Morning News* reporter, demonstrates: "Handling an infant giraffe is like tangling with a gangly. . . pile of bamboo." The sentence's rhythm and flow are advanced by the short A in *handling, giraffe, tangling, gangly and bamboo.*

Here's more assonance from Frederick Painton of *Time:* "They carry branches lopped off trees that now stand like amputees in mute supplication to the heavens." Aside from the assonance in *trees* and *amputees,* consider the consonance created by those mid-word P's in *lopped, amputees and supplication.*

Resonance resounds. Its use of N and M can lengthen or prolong a sound. Here's a lead that resonates, from the *Chicago Tribune's* Eric Zorn: "Even at the very end. . . John Gacy mouthed his banal rhetoric of denial."

And Rick Hampson of The Associated Press uses resonating N's and M's in a story about eating red meat: "New Yorkers are again sneaking off to. . . masculine bastions to consume a forbidden substance."

Often, these devices can work together to create the effect the writer seeks. Here, ten brief but suggestive words from novelist Raymond Chandler show alliteration *(slickers/shone)* as well as consonance and resonance *(rain, shone, gun)*: "In the rain, the cops' slickers shone like gun barrels."

Such devices come naturally and often unconsciously to gifted writers. But they also can be used deliberately to catch the ear. The chief hazard in using such techniques consciously rather than instinctively is that the result may be artificial. And writers must know when to stop. Too much of any of these devices makes for ridiculous reading — and the line is thin between too much and just enough. Here's one good guideline: If readers start noticing cause more than consequence, it's probably too much.

Composition

Short and choppy can damage sequence, meaning

One-sentence-per-paragraph writing is a common but unattractive convention in journalism. Such writing lacks basic organization — the grouping of information into the coherent and meaningful block of the paragraph. The style that results is less a style than a barrage of staccato, seemingly disparate, often transitionless facts. Every sentence has the same weight. No sentence seems either superior or subordinate. The work lacks dramatic pace and rhythm.

Consider the effect of such writing on the preceding paragraph:

One-sentence-per-paragraph writing is a common but unattractive convention in journalism.

Such writing lacks basic organization — the grouping of information into the coherent and meaningful block of the paragraph.

The style that results is less a style than it is a list of staccato, seemingly disparate, often transitionless facts.

Every sentence has the same weight.

No sentence seems either superior or subordinate.

The work lacks dramatic pace and rhythm.

Composition

Meaningful and seamless flow, highly prized in all prose, is requisite in good media writing. Yet newswriters often attend little to transition and shape, content with a "style" that in fact lends no style.

The one-sentence-per-paragraph convention grew out of the use of the telegraph and continued through the days of hot type, when it was easier to cut a whole paragraph than it was to excise a sentence from a paragraph. Technology has changed that, but we still see such radically shortened paragraphs — chiefly because we want to avoid long, gray blocks of type. That's a worthy goal, but it doesn't merit abandoning an element of composition so basic it's taught in grade school. Newspaper writers can paragraph more often than writers of, say, an essay or a magazine article and still shape their material. They can occasionally paragraph a single line for emphasis. But automatically hitting the return at every period is a sad substitute for purposeful story organization.

Consider the following newspaper passage:

The slap of leather and crack of wood ring through the air at Disney's Wide World of Sports complex.

It's closing in on baseball season, and the Atlanta Braves call the new complex their spring training home.

But by September, the sounds of summer will be replaced by the sound of helmets crashing into one another.

It's here that the Lamar Vikings will take on the Rutherford Rams from Panama City, Fla., in the Kaylee Scholarship Football Classic.

While the event is not new, it will be the first time it's played in Orlando.

The herky-jerkiness of one-sentence-a-paragraph writing is the main problem with that passage, but it needs editing as well as more skillful paragraphing:

Composition

Baseball's slap of leather and crack of wood resound at Disney's Wide World of Sports complex, the Atlanta Braves' new spring training home. But come September, the sound will be the clash of football helmets — when the Lamar Vikings will take on the Rutherford Rams.

The Kaylee Scholarship Football Classic is going to Orlando.

Another newspaper passage:

Ted Somers Jr. told his son not to go into farming.

But William Somers had his heart set on the fields and barns.

He took the operation — near Ridge and Fowler roads in Brady Township, where his father had once milked dairy cows — and built on it.

He nurtured it.

And he expanded it to more than 2,000 acres from the 160 his father once worked.

As his children grew, he and his wife, Rebecca, told them they didn't have to stick with the family farm.

'We never pushed the farm onto our kids,' says Rebecca Somers, president of the Saginaw County Farm Bureau.

'It's a hard life, and if your heart's not in it, you're not going to be successful.'

Two of their sons followed their father into the fields.

And they've followed both their parents into leadership positions in the farming community.

The Somers brothers are among the next generation of Michigan's farmers — college educated, active in agriculture and active in the community.

Composition

Now look at the effect of thoughtful paragraphing (and light editing):

William Somers' dad told him not to go into farming. But William's heart was set on fields and barns, so he took over the family farm near Ridge and Fowler roads in Brady Township.

He built and nurtured the farm, eventually expanding its 160 acres to more than 2,000. And as his children grew, William — like his father before him — told them they didn't have to stay with the farm.

'We never pushed the farm onto our kids,' says William's wife, Rebecca, president of the Saginaw County Farm Bureau. 'It's a hard life, and if your heart's not in it, you're not going to be successful.'

'But two of the Somers boys followed their father into the fields, just as they've followed him into leadership positions in the farming community. The brothers are among the next generation of Michigan's farmers — college educated, active in agriculture and in the community.'

When we think or write, we form ideas sequentially and through association — a sequence and association that in turn promote reader understanding. Wrenching sentences from their most coherent setting — the paragraph — and presenting them in artificial isolation damages coherence and polish.

Attribution, she said

Overuse and tense problems get in the story's way

An unattractive feature of some newswriting is needless or repetitive attribution. Particularly annoying is a style that attributes almost every sentence. We should document whatever must be documented, of course, but gracefully — in a way that doesn't assault the reader's ear.

In other words, an attribution problem is just another writing problem. Skillful writers craft seamless sentences in which attribution is as purposeful and invisible as any other device.

Take, for example, a complex breaking story with lots of quotations and detail — a prison riot and escape, say. We could top that story with a summary lead and then write a pivotal paragraph such as: "Police gave the following account of the breakout." That approach would allow us to tell a story, without slavishly attributing every sentence.

Stick to plain and neutral verbs of attribution. *Said* is safe and, unless badly overworked, unobtrusive. *Stated* or *added* can work if you've overused *said*. *Explained* and *announced* are fine if the source really is explaining or announcing. Avoid the weird (*opined, averred, snorted, laughed, chuckled, uttered, voiced, shrugged*), the slanted *(claimed)*, or the overly emphatic *(declared, proclaimed)*.

Here's an over-attributed passage (the names of the principals and the county are changed):

> *LaRue **said** the deputies' first mistake was not making sure they were raiding the right house after they got a tip from an informant. He **said** the water company told authorities that Ms. Jones— not the drug suspects — lived in the home, but deputies raided anyway.*
>
> *Deputies also continued to search the women even after one officer recognized Ms. Smith and realized they had the wrong address, LaRue **said**.*
>
> *'They're not required to never make a mistake,' he **said**. 'There are certain guidelines that are in place. . . because there's going to be accidents with snitches.'*
>
> *Sheriff Hicks **said** he believes his deputies acted appropriately. But they were given bad information, he **said**, that they tried to verify several times.*
>
> *A strip search is standard in drug raids for deputies' safety, Hicks **said**. When no drugs or weapons were found on the women, deputies promptly left the house without searching it, he **said**.*
>
> *'It was a matter of miscommunication,' he **said**. 'I don't think it was handled badly at all.'*

The revision below documents as necessary, but reduces the number of attributions.

> *The deputies' first mistake, said LaRue, was raiding the house even after authorities had been told that Ms. Jones — not the drug suspects — lived there. Then they'd compounded the error, he added, by continuing to search the women after an officer recognized Ms. Smith and realized they were in the wrong house.*

Strip searches are standard safety measures in Kipp County drug raids. Sheriff Hicks said he thought his officers had acted appropriately, but on false information — which they had tried several times to verify. When no drugs or weapons were found on the women, he added, the deputies promptly left the house without searching it.

That revision also fixes other problems in the passage, as follows.

Cut the first quotation; it's neither clear nor pertinent. Don't confuse weird or dumb quotes with *good* quotes. (Weird and dumb quotes *can* be good quotes, depending upon the story and its purpose, but that's another subject. For now, let's just say that this story has serious intent and is simply trying to inform, so the quotes should mesh and have the same purpose.) Attorney LaRue's *there's going to be accidents with snitches* is as odd as it is ungrammatical. *They're not required to never make a mistake:* Split infinitives are not wrong, but they can be hideous, and this one is. *There are certain guidelines that are in place:* Good thing, because guidelines that are *not* "in place" aren't worth much.

The passage also has sequence-of-tense problems, common in newswriting. When a past-tense sentence includes something that happened even earlier, use the past-perfect *had:*

Not: said he thought his officers acted appropriately.

But: said he thought his officers *had* acted appropriately.

Let the first or main verb set the tense. If it's in past tense, other verbs will be past, past perfect or conditional.

*Not: said he **believes**.*

*But: said he **believed**.*

*Not: said he **will** go.*

*But: said he **would** go.*

Verbs accompanying the present-tense *says* should also be present tense: *says he believes; says he will go.*

Attribution, she said.

Newswriting contains many past-plus-present tense errors, in part because we seem confused about what constitutes a universal statement. "He *said* the proposal *will*" should be "said the proposal *would*." "She *said* she is going to Tibet" should be "said she *was* going to Tibet." It's true that universal statements occasionally are exceptions to sequence-of-tense rules, but only if the past tense is clumsy or misleading. For example: "He explained why the sky *appears* to be blue." *Appears* is better in this case, even though the sentence is in past tense, because *appeared* could make it seem that the sky appeared to be blue only at that time. In the sentence, "She *said* she *was* going to Tibet," the *was* is correct even though she is still going to Tibet. Her going to Tibet is not a *universal* statement; it's merely a statement that is still true.

36

Quotations: The spice of write

Paraphrasing is the lost art of pruning quotes

Good journalism thrives on good quotations. The right quotes, carefully selected and presented, enliven and humanize a story and help make it clear, credible, immediate and dramatic.

Yet many quotations in journalism are dull, repetitive, ill-phrased, ungrammatical, nonsensical, self-serving or just plain dumb. We try to buttress stories with a source's exact words even when those words are weak rather than strong.

We're not talking about the crazy but memorable quote. Those qualify as good quotes whatever else they may be. Happily, there was a reporter around when Gerald Ford said: *If President Lincoln were alive today, he'd roll over in his grave.* We're glad somebody recorded it when former Mayor Richard Daley said during the 1968 Democratic Convention riots in Chicago: *The policeman isn't there to create disorder. He's there to preserve disorder.* And we can be grateful someone quoted another great example of political bafflegab: *Mr. Speaker, I smell a rat. I see him forming in the air. But I'll nip him in the bud.*

Such quotes are good even if flawed. They're strong and enormously entertaining. We don't need fewer of those. We need fewer of the boring, wordy, jargon-laden and pretentious quotes that journalism is heir to. Quotes like this:

'Although many people recognize the allure of it, I think it's very important to recognize that the pharmacological effects are only one component of an end result of some kind of want and addiction. For any substance, the user's own expectations and attitudes, mind set, in conjunction with the social circumstances combine to produce the outcome,' she said.

Paraphrasing and Pruning

Quotations should help us understand the story. Somebody should say the right things in the right way. If the sources don't, the writer must. That means translating — paraphrasing — to make clear, bright, undistorted and emphatic points. That didn't happen in the quotation above, and it doesn't happen in the quotation below.

'Samples of clonidine hydrochloride 0.3 milligram tablets submitted for bioequivalence testing by Interpharm were not the same as the product on the market,' the agency said.

The problem is obvious. We cover a beat. We hear lots of this kind of stuff. And after a while, it starts to sound like. . . well, like *English*.

But we shouldn't make the reader do our job of translating and interpreting. The reporter's job is to be an intelligent mediator, not just a tape recorder. We must know the subject in order to translate, of course, as well as to avoid slavishly including incorrect or misleading quotations or paraphrases. Take the following:

Government officials warn that the nation's production of such toxic wastes as PCBs and dioxins is far outstripping its ability to dispose of them safely and efficiently.

The problem? Production of PCBs has been banned since the late '70s and no one *produces* dioxin. It's a byproduct in the creation of paper and many common chemical products. So if this writer's sources knew neither that PCBs are banned nor that nobody "produces" dioxins, they're hardly informed sources.

Or the sources are not accurately paraphrased.

"But That's What They Said"

The point is that everything in our publication is in our publication. If the stories are literate, coherent and interesting, the tone of the whole will be raised and the work will seem intelligent and responsible. On the other hand, if the stories are littered with ungrammatical, silly, inaccurate or illogical expression, the whole work will be debased.

We can't change quotes. But we can prune, and we can paraphrase. And while it isn't our job to correct quotations or to make people seem smarter or more eloquent than they are, it *is* our job to craft polished stories. We should use quotations to that end. (There are, of course, cases in which we have fair reason to expose ignorance or illiteracy. That's another subject.)

Here's a typical newspaper passage in which the readers are forced to plow through one meaningless word after another:

'I am a healing force,' he said in his office Thursday after meeting with reporters. 'I have built a reputation as a consensus builder, a coalition builder. . . . The way to become a healing force is to build a consensus, respect the views of others. You can't shout and call names. That's what I call a healing force and that's me.'

What can be done? We can find the necessary words and cut the others (including the ungrammatical "that's *me*"):

'I am a healing force,' he said Thursday. 'The way to become a healing force is to build a consensus, respect the views of others. You can't snout and call names.'

Now, some might say: "Aren't you doing a service by showing what a blowhard this guy is?" But that's a little subtle. If we want the readers to know something about someone, we should find someone to say or suggest it. Then the supporting quotes would mean something. But we can't expect the readers to *divine* the message between the lines. In most newswriting, a broadsword works better than a stiletto.

Of course, certain odd or incomprehensible quotes *do* show the audience something important about the speaker. Such quotations add information, dimension and even delight to a story. For example, Jesse Jackson's love for rhetoric and metaphor are both clear and amusing in: *If we crush the grapes of hope into raisins of despair, they may not be able to bounce back in the fall.* We learn something about Dan Quayle when we read that he said the Holocaust was "an obscene period in our nation's history." That's a telling if mystifying quote.

Weak quotes, though, tell us little or nothing. Yet we commonly defend them: "Well, that's what they said." That's an abdication of responsibility. Shaping the material is the writer's job. The best writers didn't get that way by shoveling blather into their copy just because somebody said it.

Quote Leads: A Failed Device

Just finding lively, accurate and interesting quotations isn't the end of the problem. We also must decide how best to present them. And the worst place to present them is at the beginning. Most quote leads are easy, lazy and lousy. They have no context. The readers don't know who's speaking, why, or what about. And without context, even the best quotes are wasted.

Bad as they usually are, though, quote leads still appear regularly in newspapers. Say someone approaches us and blurts: "The priest said a forest grows in silence, but when a tree falls, it thunders to the ground." We're going to ask that person one of several questions: 1) *What are you talking about?* 2) *Is something wrong with you?* 3) *Are you Kahlil Gibran or Mortimer Snerd?*

This speaker's approach breaks one of the basic tenets of storytelling: It begins without a beginning. It fails to offer the information we need to understand — and of course we immediately clamor for context.

Television can make quote beginnings work, but the practice is uncertain even there. The speaker's face and voice must be recognizable and the words brief, attention-getting and self-explanatory. If not, it's best to start with a few words of identification, background and explanation. In both radio and print, however, quote leads are confusing or annoying or both. Those media need a framework for the speaker's words. Otherwise, some anonymous person is saying obscure things about some uncertain subject. Here, again, is that forest/tree quotation and the original newspaper lead in which it appeared.

'A forest grows in silence,' said the Melanesian Catholic priest. 'But when a tree falls, it thunders to the ground.'
His words were punctuated by women sobbing. Then he murmured, 'A big tree has fallen.'

That unfortunate lead tops a story about the murder of an important figure on the island of New Caledonia. It tries to be mournful and respectful, but its incantation-like words come to the reader cold and may inspire guffaws instead of sympathy. Yet if we prune the quote a little and take the time to set it up, we can dignify the subject:

Hundreds of New Caledonia islanders trekked to a remote mountain village last week to salute their slain leader, Jean-Marie Tjibaou.

A Melanesian Catholic priest led the memorial service, held in Tiendanite, a village in the French South Pacific territory.

'When a tree falls, it thunders to the ground,' the priest said, his words punctuated by the mourners' sobs. 'A big tree has fallen.'

Often, we can repair quote leads simply by putting the quotation after the material in the second paragraph.

'Show me the way, show me the way, show me the way.'

Down the long stretch where so many Kentucky Derby dreams had died, trainer Nick Zito kept chanting those words as Strike the Gold provided the realization of that dream by showing 15 followers the way to the wire.

The second graf could set up the quote:

Strike the Gold pounded down that long stretch Saturday where so many Kentucky Derby dreams had died, and trainer Nick Zito chanted. 'Show me the way, show me the way, show me the way.'

Another Quote Lead Problem: Getting Out Of It

Quote leads create transition problems, too. Watch the writers below struggle unsuccessfully to get from the quotation into the story.

'The idea of the book was to take a major poet and shove him up a major river.'

That is how Redmond O'Hanlon describes Into the Heart of Borneo, *his account of the journey he made with James Fenton, an English poet, up the Rajang River into primal, bug-infested jungle.*

'This is really not good.'
The speaker was Barbara Lewis, 38, a mother of two who lives in Libertyville, Ill., and she was responding to something she had read in the newspaper.

'Gee,' the NHL scout was saying, 'I really wish you weren't going to write about him. I was kind of hoping nobody would find out about him.'
'Him' would be Peter Ambroziak.

The first lead has the usual awkward pivot: "That is how Redmond O'Hanlon describes. . . ." The second faces a similar problem, but the opening quote ("This is really not good.") is so weak we wonder why the writer used it at all. The third is reduced to phrasing as ungrammatical as it is awkward: "*Him* would be Peter Ambroziak."

Quote Fragments

Quote leads aren't the only mistake we make in presenting quotations — just the most obvious. The fragmented quote also presents special problems. We fragment quotes sensibly only when the words are inflammatory, provocative, figures of speech, or slang. Yet we read, for example, that Smith said he would talk to the governor in "a couple of weeks." We should avoid such innocuous and neutral fragments.

Quotations: The spice of write

In a question and answer session with the Magazine Publishers of America, he called the . . . (projected deficit) 'disturbing.' and said he would prod Congressional leaders to forge a budget 'in the next couple of weeks.'

There's more wrong here than the fragments, but at the very least, the writer might have paraphrased throughout instead of disrupting the passage with fragments, ellipses and parentheses.

A further flaw is the habit of repeating a quote's essence in the set-up. Careful writers usually rephrase the speaker's words, but there's still a duplication of idea, so the quotes seem flat and repetitive. Every sentence in the story should move the story forward. So we should borrow only enough from the quote to get into it, trim what we've borrowed if possible and serve something fresh in both set-up paragraph and quote. The passage below runs in place:

Analysts said the report was not surprising considering the employment cuts and falling incomes accompanying a recession.

'It is consistent with retail sales being weak, with the decline in the employment numbers and personal incomes,' said economist John Silva.

Cutting is the answer. Trim "considering the employment cuts and falling incomes." The source makes both points — no reason to make them twice. That would leave us with: "Analysts said the report was not surprising during a recession." That's a good way to get into the quote, which will now seem more meaningful because it's not repetitious.

Another common mechanical problem with fragmented quotes is switching pronouns in narrative and quote. We read, for example: "Smith said *he* had 'only *myself* to blame.'" The solution to such oddities is a solid paraphrase or more skillful fragmenting.

Quotations: The spice of write

Here's the problem in action:

If Iraqi forces were to use chemical weapons, he said, 'I think we'd take action directly against those forces. . . in a limited way, but in a very decisive way.'

The fix? A straight and graceful paraphrase:

He said he thought that if Iraq used chemical weapons, the United States would take limited but direct action.

Fast, fluid and graceful flow is key to good writing — and to good story-telling. Quotations should be integrated into the flow of the narrative so they become part of a seamless whole.

37

Language skill and credibility

Mistakes make readers doubt

Media credibility is a big issue at the moment, with most of the discussion touching on such concerns as shoddy reporting or outright fabrication. We hear less, however, about another offense to credibility that immediately impairs the journalist's authority and the reader's trust. That offense is second-rate language skill.

I know of no other profession that has at its command only one tool and yet has such giddy disregard of that tool's proper use. Wordsmiths should know words, surely: Between writer and reader stands only the language, and its skillful use should be a given. When lawyers are ignorant of law, doctors of medicine, cooks of food, carpenters of hammer and nail, gardeners of growing things — all lose their practices. There's no such consequence for reporters and editors, but the cost to their medium is high. Shoddy expression is a constant source of reader distress — and ultimately distrust.

We're talking in part about grammar, punctuation, structure, spelling — subjects this column has often addressed. But beyond form, there's that all-important matter of content. Examples:

"Police recovered anti-suppressant drugs in a container without a prescription." "Recovered," police jargon for *discovered* or *found*, actually means to get back, regain, repossess, reclaim. But what could "anti-suppressant" mean? To suppress the suppressant? "Without a prescription" seems to refer to the officers' "recovery" rather than to the drugs. Better: "Police found unprescribed anti-depressant drugs in an unmarked container."

"She deserves yet another kudo for her persistence." There's no such thing as one kudo. *Kudos*, which means glory or fame, is sin-gular. Better: "She deserves kudos for her persistence as well."

"He looks younger than 35. He looks more like Frankie Avalon." If he looks more like Frankie Avalon than 35, then he looks more like 60.

"Michael stayed in their mansion, where he ate, slept and swam in the family pool." This must be what people mean when they say they *live* in the pool.

"Flanagan later confided that he 'hates Memphis' and 'hates country music.'" *Ah hates Memphis; Ah hates country music?* Proficient handling of quotations is vital to narrative polish. Those fragmented quotes cannot be correct. The writer has changed the verb to agree with *he* rather than I. Paraphrase: "Flanagan later con-fided that he hated Memphis and hated country music."

"Fans may remember 'Beyond the Fringe,' from whence the team originated." Careful writers avoid the redundant "from whence." *Whence* means "from where," just as *thence* means "from there."

"A plane believed to be leaving Redbird Airport en route to Corpus Christi was reported missing Monday evening." A plane "believed to be leaving" the airport was reported missing? Is the plane missing from the runway, then? If we assume a tense problem and read "believed to be leaving" as "believed to have left," things get more ridiculous. Did it leave or not? If not, maybe it's not even missing — hooray! Clearer: "A plane believed to be en route to Corpus Christi. . . ."

"The governor's slight-of-hand reputation is enhanced by his handling of appointments." The governor has small hands? Make it *sleight*-of-hand. Also, the repetition of *hand* and *handling* is ham-handed, so to speak.

"Pus still oozed from the unhealed wounds of the Black Hawk Indian War as young James entered boyhood." Gag us with a metaphor.

"The actor doesn't seem present at times, so we wonder, as well: 'Wherefore art thou, Romeo?' " *Wherefore* means why or for that reason — not *where*. Juliet is not asking "*where* are you, Romeo," but "*why* are you Romeo?" She laments that he bears the name of the family enemy, which is clear from her celebrated words: "Wherefore art thou Romeo? Deny thy father and refuse thy name."

"She said she has known of her telepathic powers since childhood, when she correctly foretold events." Foretelling events is precognition, not telepathy. Telepathy is mind-reading or thought transference.

"Hooray! The Frost Belt is unthawing." If it's *unthawed*, then it must be refrozen.

"Now he prefers to live, as Thomas Gray wrote, far from the maddening crowd." Gray actually wrote "far from the *madding* crowd." *Madding* means tumultuous or restless, an import wholly different from *maddening*.

Must we be perfect? Perfection is unreachable, but that goal is the only way to keep our standards as high as they must be to serve our audience. Although the reader's intelligence is often maligned in newsrooms, that's an attitude as misinformed as it is arrogant. Newspaper readers comprise the country's *most* educated people, and we should strive to be at least as smart as they. Mistakes will surely happen, despite our best efforts, and most readers will forgive occasional errors quickly and candidly corrected. But that fact should make us more, not less, diligent. The mistakes the readers find hard to forgive and that ultimately destroy our credibility are those that seem to occur either because we don't know or because we don't care.

column

38

Avoiding pronoun pitfalls

When in doubt about *who* or *whom*, try a substitution

Problems with pronouns cause some of our most common gram-matical gaffes. Consider:

"She's older than *him*."

"They gave the reports to Smith, Jones and *myself.*"

"This is between you and *I*."

"They want to talk to *whomever* is there."

"The Acme *Company* will move *their* warehouse to their new location in June."

"*Anyone* who thinks *they* could be a professional golfer should talk to him."

The form of pronoun needed depends upon whether it is a sub-ject or object in the sentence. If it's a subject, it acts: *I, he, she, they, we, who,* for example. And if it's an object, it receives the action: *me, him, her, them, us, whom,* for example. "Self" pronouns are neither subjects nor objects but reflexives (*I hurt myself*) or intensifiers (*they* are all going, but I *myself* am staying home).

"She's older than him" actually says: "She's older than he *is*." So we need the subject *he* for the verb *is* — even though the verb is understood rather than spoken. (We would not say "older than *him* is.") Corrected: "She's older than he."

If we remove Smith and Jones from "They gave the reports to Smith, Jones and myself," we see right away that we need an object — not "gave the reports to *myself*," but "gave the reports to *me*." Corrected: "They gave the reports to Smith, Jones and me."

We often can find out if we need a subjective or objective pronoun by substituting some other pronoun. For example: "This is between you and I." Remove *you and I* and use other pronouns: "This is between *we*, between *they*, between *us*, between *them*." Again, we see that the subject *we* or *they* is wrong and the object *us* or *them* is right. So we'd need the objective *me*: "This is between you and me."

The substitution game is useful, as well, in settling *who/whom* questions. (*Who* is the subject, *whom* the object.) Nobody has a problem with "Who called?" But change that to "Who did you say called," and many want to make it *whom*. Yet it's the same sort of sentence: "You did say *she, he, they* called?" Again, pronoun substitution shows that we need the subject *who*, not the object *whom* — we would not say "You did say *him* called?"

"They want to talk to *whomever* is there": The correct choice is *whoever*. Such sentences are confusing because we want an object for *talk to*, yet we also need a subject for *is there*. In such sentences, the subjective pronoun wins, and the whole clause (in this case, *whoever is there*) is the object. Corrected: "They want to talk to whoever is there."

"The Acme Company will move their warehouse to their new location in June": Collective nouns (for example: *class, group, family, committee, team, company*) are usually singular in American English. The Acme Company is an "it" (but never "it's," which is not possessive and means *it is*). *Anyone, everyone, no one, anybody, everybody, nobody*, and *each* also are singular. Corrected: "The Acme Company will move its warehouse to its new location in June."

"*Anyone* who thinks *they* could be a professional golfer should talk to him" should be recast to fix the "anyone/they" agreement problem. If we keep the singular antecedent *anyone*, a singular pronoun must follow. Should we use *he* or *she*, or should we stick to *he*? In fact, both are awkward and create problems of their own. "He or she" is bulky and awkward. *He* creates a gender problem that offends many, and avoiding offense is sensible if we want to keep the message from getting lost in irrelevancies. (Some adherents to political correctness say go ahead and use *anyone/they;* that a grammatical error is preferable to sexism. This is a flawed practice. Most readers will not assume that the error is a political statement — which itself may offend — but that the writer is ignorant.)

We can make the antecedent *anyone* plural, however: "Golfers who think they could be professional should talk to him." This version satisfies all demands, whether of grace, grammar or political correctness.

Not all grammatical errors involve pronouns, of course. But pronouns cause so much confusion that mastering them will clear up a good deal of confusion in our communications.

Comma sense

Common comma causes uncommon problems

The comma, basic as it is, can cause great confusion even among professional writers. Media writers do seem to have mastered one simple comma rule that eludes many — that in American English, commas go *inside* quotation marks. Beyond that principle, inconsistency reigns.

A common error arises when placing commas between adjectives preceding a noun:

- *His only memory of those freaky San Francisco years was a pale yellow, wood-frame house.*
- *She was an old, gray mare of a person, horse-faced and heavy-boned.*
- *He was a charming, young reprobate.*

Commas should not follow *yellow, old* or *charming. Pale yellow* modifies *wood-frame house* — not just *house. Old* modifies *gray mare* — not just *mare.* And *charming* modifies *young reprobate.* We shouldn't automatically insert commas between multiple adjectives before a noun because those adjectives may not be separate and equal modifiers. Sometimes, as we see in the examples above, the adjective modifies a *group* of words rather than just the noun.

Comma sense

Here's a great little trick if you're unsure about placing a comma between adjectives. Try the conjunction *and* where the comma would go: yellow *and* wood-frame house, old *and* gray mare, charming *and* young reprobate. If the *and* sounds odd — as those do — don't use a comma. The awkwardness of the conjunction shows that the adjectives are not separate and equal modifiers. Test the correctness of the examples below by placing an *and* after *turreted, beautiful* and *limp.* You'll see instantly that commas should not separate those adjectives from the adjectives that follow.

- *The turreted red brick tower.*
- *The beautiful infant girl.*
- *Her limp white wrist.*

Now consider the phrasing a *large, ugly dog.* We can verify the need for a comma because *a large and ugly dog* sounds fine. More examples:

- *His broad, guileless smile showed an octave of strong, healthy teeth* (his broad *and* guileless smile; strong *and* healthy teeth).
- *They entered the old, dilapidated house* (the old *and* dilapidated house).
- *Babies are lovable, cuddly neurotics* (lovable *and* cuddly).

Another common comma problem concerns two clauses joined with a conjunction. We place a comma before the conjunction when both clauses are independent:

- *I don't try to do my secretary's job, and she doesn't either.*
- *Ring Lardner said he knew what it was to be hungry, but he always went right to a restaurant.*
- *He who hesitates is not only lost, but he also just missed his exit.*

We omit the comma, however, when joining certain independent and *dependent* clauses with a conjunction — that is, when two or more verbs have the same subject:

- *He hurled himself from the room and ran off madly in all directions.*
- *I received your letter and will waste no time reading it.*
- *Technological progress might have been OK once but has gone on far too long.*

Remember that the comma goes *before* the conjunction, though. We often see commas following *but* or *and*, especially at the beginning of a sentence: *And, the council simply refused to listen. But, the council simply refused to listen.* Those commas are unnecessary unless they're punctuating something else in the sentence, such as the parenthetical attribution in this example: *But, according to news reports, the council simply refused to listen.*

Appositives also cause comma problems. We use commas to set off appositives (words that identify a preceding noun or pronoun) that aren't essential but add parenthetical information:

- *Her husband, Paul, eats raw meat, even as it quivers on the plate.*
- *My neighbor, a thief, is said to help himself because he can't help himself.*
- *Her laugh, a bray fit for a donkey, echoed through the room.*

But the commas are omitted with appositives that are essential or restrictive:

- *He visited his sister Mary on his return from Europe.*
- *Dostoevsky's novel* Crime and Punishment *is considered one of literature's first psychological works.*

In the first example above, it would be correct to place commas around *Mary* if she were the subject's only sister. Likewise, commas would correctly surround *Crime and Punishment* if Dostoevsky had written only one novel.

Introductory clauses and phrases also cause confusion. That's in part because very short and simple introductory structures can get by without a comma: *At sunrise the churchbells rang. In the evenings we drank ourselves into oblivion.* But it's not *wrong* to follow even such short beginning phrases with commas. And clarity and balance usually demand a comma after longer or more involved introductory clauses or phrases:

- *After all is said and done, more is said than done.*
- *If you drink a pint of milk every day for 1200 months, you'll be about 100.*
- *If you like to be the center of attention, start a fistfight.*

However, an adverbial clause appearing in the middle of a sentence — between subject and verb — has not one but two commas. And it shouldn't lose either of them:

- *Gunther, in his tiresome way, slipped into and out of a coma several times during the board meeting.*
- *Gianni "The Nose" DeSico, when asked if he was a Christian, replied, "Yeah, sure. Now beat it."*
- *Members of the new alliance, before a public hearing, announced that the purpose of a committee was to spread the blame.*

In short, the correctly executed comma has its reasons. If a sentence seems busy with commas, it's better to recast it than to pluck out its punctuation.

40

Editing the wire I

Formula writing can be habit-forming

Here's proof — if we needed it — that wire writing can be terrible:

After months of making many promises but offering few specifics, Republican senators on Tuesday proposed a historic plan that showed in actual dollars and cents how they hope to balance the federal budget.

The plan calls for cuts in projected government spending of nearly $1 trillion over the next seven years.

Reporters and editors get so used to this sort of writing that they no longer see how unreadable it is. But here's that lead, simply edited:

Republican senators presented a plan Tuesday showing exactly how they hope to balance the budget. The proposal follows months of promises but few specifics and includes cuts of nearly a trillion dollars over the next seven years.

No one ever said editing on deadline was easy. But weak writing so often shows certain characteristics that editing becomes easier once we know what we're looking for. The original lead is weak because it's formula journalism.

■ It misplaces the time element.

■ It's choked with hackneyed, careless and inflated expression.

■ It backs in with a dependent clause.

Time. The unnatural habit of placing the time element before the verb is an unhappy and formulaic practice. We don't talk that way (*I at noon will eat lunch*) and shouldn't write that way unless we have no other choice.

Hackneyed, careless and inflated expression. "Actual" dollars and cents? As opposed to *imaginary* dollars and cents? Cuts in "projected" spending? Of course it's projected, since 1) you can't cut what you've already spent, and 2) the cuts are to be made over the next seven years.

Further, those senators didn't propose a "historic" plan. They merely proposed a plan. A plan can't be historic unless it's adopted, and even then, only time will tell.

Formula journalism is full of the sort of forced excitement seen in *historic*. What it means is *this exact plan hasn't been presented before* — in other words, it's *new*. Although news is the business of journalism, journalists often seem surprised by it.

We see the same sort of clichéd and contrived drama in expressions such as *unprecedented* (Wow! First time!) or *for the second time in as many years* (Zowie! Twice!). Spectators are *horrified*, rivers *rampage*, developments are *stunning*, people are *reeling*, *grisly* murders often occur in *densely wooded lots*. People are *assailed*; others *lash out*. Some *strongman* retreats to his *sprawling estate* while sources *on the ground* report that the conflict is *escalating*. If there's a coup, it will be *bloody*. Or *bloodless*.

In journalese, the news is tricked out in gaud, and solid, meaningful words become so much tinsel. Hack writers never seem to learn that hyperbole reduces rather than enlarges.

Backing in. We back in when we begin a lead with a preposition, verb, verbal, or certain conjunctions and adverbs. Such sentences are easy to recognize because they begin with a dependent clause or phrase rather than with the sentence's *subject*. Readers learn some corollary thing about the subject before they even know the subject. The backed-in action is disembodied, with nobody performing it. Or background and explanation comes before we know the sentence's topic.

Not every backed-in beginning is bad. Short introductory phrases and clauses are fine (*a decade ago, last year, during the meeting*). Most lead sentences simply are better, however, if we begin with a subject. At the beginning, the readers don't know what the story's about, and a subject anchors the story for them.

Here are further examples of formulaic wire writing and deadline fixes that create livelier, more story-telling beginnings.

Original: *In a step the Clinton administration hailed as 'a gift to next generations,' most countries of the world agreed Thursday to make permanent the 25-year-old treaty banning the spread of nuclear arms.*

Support for the U.S.-backed, indefinite renewal of the Nuclear Nonproliferation Treaty was so overwhelming that. . . .

Problems: Again, we have backing in and journalese (*hailed*). Add to that an equally formulaic and unreadable pile-up of adjectives: "U.S.-backed, indefinite renewal of the Nuclear Nonproliferation Treaty."

Edited: *Most nations agreed Thursday to make permanent the 25-year-old pact banning the spread of nuclear arms. The Clinton administration said the Nuclear Nonproliferation Treaty was a gift to future generations.*

Original: *As the Bosnian crisis escalated dangerously, NATO members' defense ministers Saturday announced plans for a strongly armed rapid response unit that will be charged with adding military might to the embattled United Nations peacekeeping force in Bosnia-Herzegovina.*

Editing the wire I

Problems: Backing in. Journalese: *escalated dangerously, embattled, military might.* Adjective pile-up: "strongly armed rapid response unit."

Edited: *A heavily armed special unit will supplement the U.N. peacekeeper effort in Bosnia-Herzegovina, NATO said Saturday. The Bosnian crisis worsened Friday when. . . .*

Original: *President Clinton said Friday that the U.S. policy to limit America's military role in Bosnia-Herzegovina 'remains firm' despite the downing of a U.S. fighter jet by Bosnian Serbs.*

Problems: This lead would be fine without the quotation marks. Formula writers often stud leads with unnecessary quote fragments. "Remains firm" is garden-variety language, as easily ours as the speaker's. The whole quote doubtless will be lower in the story; why fragment it here? Save quotation marks for incendiary, figurative, ironic or colloquial fragments.

We should edit copy from the wire as carefully as we edit copy from the staff. Most readers don't distinguish between wire and staff copy, nor should they. Simply said, everything that's in our newspaper is in our newspaper, and readers judge it on its entirety.

column

41

Editing the wire II

Wire editors shouldn't assume perfect readiness of wire copy

Rushed editors often don't give wire stories the attention they need. *Well, wire copy is usually written by experienced journalists,* the reasoning goes, *and it's already been edited.* But much of the unreadable writing, journalese and formula in newspapers is in wire stories.

It's not unusual, of course, to find fine writing on the wires, but we shouldn't *assume* its superiority. It also isn't unusual to find clear, graceful staff writing and unclear, clunky wire writing in the same newspaper. In such cases, the wire copy obviously isn't subject to the same writing standards as staff copy.

Here are two wire stories that appeared in many newspapers. In each case, would the editors at those newspapers have accepted such a mélange from a staff reporter?

Original: *Spurred by a need to salve economic wounds at home, Japanese investors have sharply accelerated their retreat from the U.S. real estate market they galloped into last decade, said a study released Thursday.*

Problems: Backing in with a dependent clause instead of starting with a subject fusses up the writing. Journalese dulls its meaning: *spurred, salve economic wounds, sharply accelerated.* Weird phrasing and runaway metaphor make the passage laughable: Ponder "accelerating a retreat," for example. And the horsy images of "spurred" and "galloped" don't mesh with "salving wounds" and "accelerating." A little careful editing helps:

Edited: *Japanese investors are leaving the U.S. real estate market in the '90s almost as fast as they entered it in the '80s, said a study released Thursday. The investors, influenced by economic distress at home. . . .*

Original: *A political scenario as unstable as Boris Yeltsin's malfunctioning heart began materializing here Friday, as doctors said the hospitalized Russian president must undergo five weeks of intensive monitoring.*

Despite announcing that Yeltsin still suffered an unstable blood supply to his heart. . . .

Problems: This passage manages at once to be both overwritten and vague. The strained wordplay doesn't help — the *malfunctioning heart,* the *unstable blood supply* and the *unstable political scenario.* Worse, that political scenario began "materializing" in Moscow Monday. Shades of Lord Bulwer-Lytton.

Edited: *Boris Yeltsin's prolonged hospital stay is further unsettling already shaky Russian politics. Doctors announced Friday that the blood supply to Yeltsin's heart was unstable and that he must be carefully monitored for five more weeks.*

Wire stories can be littered with wordy, say-nothing quotations that attentive editors can easily prune or paraphrase, witness this newspaper passage:

Original: *"I am a healing force" he said in his office Thursday after meeting with reporters. "I have built a reputation as a consensus* *builder, a coalition builder. . . . The way to become a healing force is to build a consensus, respect the views of others. You can't shout and call names. That's what I call a healing force and that's me."*

Problems: The readers are forced to plow through one meaningless word after another. What can be done? We can find the necessary words and cut the others:

Edited: *'I am a healing force,' he said Thursday. 'The way to become a healing force is to build a consensus, respect the views of others. You can't shout and call names.'*

Another common writing problem in wire stories is the long and busy opening sentence that seeks to make too many points:

Original: *Stunned Israelis by the hundreds of thousands paid final respects today to their fallen leader, Yitzhak Rabin, lighting candles on the square where he was slain, praying at the Western Wall, and filing through the afternoon and into the night past his simple soldier's coffin, wrapped in an Israeli flag.*

Problems: The writing is loose and awkward. A careful editor could provide more information and improve grace and clarity through tightening and shorter sentences.

Edited: *Hundreds of thousands of Israelis paid final tribute today to Prime Minister Yitzhak Rabin, who was assassinated Saturday in Tel Aviv. Stunned mourners lit candles on the square where their leader was slain, prayed at the Western Wall, and filed steadily past the simple soldier's coffin, wrapped in an Israeli flag.*

Some wire copy, of course, suffers missing information or organization problems that cannot be solved quickly by a newspaper's wire editors. Those are special problems that should be taken up with the wire service. But the all-too-common problems of journalese, wordiness, length, density and backing in are easily remedied — and should be.

42

Taking risks

Why should you? Good writing is safe writing

Writing counselors often advise writers to "take risks." That glib expression is a constant at writing workshops or wherever writing gurus get together. Seldom do concrete examples of "risk-taking" newswriting accompany that advice — but when they do, they invariably exemplify good, not necessarily *risky*, writing.

James Joyce took risks. William Faulkner took risks. Both sought to innovate, to create new forms. William and Henry James took risks — with the result that one wrote psychology as if it were fiction, and the other wrote fiction as if it were psychology. All gambled. But that they *gambled* is not what made them good writers.

Tellingly, none wrote for the news media. Neither their work nor their particular kind of risk belongs in the news, welcome as it is elsewhere.

Beyond that, isn't it a little weird that finding a way to write fresh, clear and interesting stories means "taking a risk"? What's the big gamble in that? Want a *real* risk? Continue to bore, baffle and annoy the readers with the dull, fuzzy and formulaic stuff glutting today's newswriting. There's the real risk:

"A year ago, citing a heavy burden of administrative red tape, the

Social Security Administration mandated in a rare move a reduction in the kind and amount of paperwork its employers were required to do by ordering its employees to produce more paperwork."

That same lead as it's rendered below is not risky. It's a sure thing because it's fresh, interesting and intelligent — good writing from Doug Swanson of *The Dallas Morning News*:

Last year the Social Security Administration sought to reduce its paperwork. To do so, it ordered the printing of 15 million pieces of paper.

Risky and trite:

"Pressed for cash and unable to pay her tuition, university student Heidi Mattson, a petite, blond 20-year-old minister's daughter, has been bumping and grinding her way through school strip-dancing in a local nightclub."

A sure thing, from Florence Shinkle of the *St. Louis Post-Dispatch*:

Whose polished flank is that in the smoky circle of stage light? It's Heavenly Heidi, Heidi Mattson, another underfunded student working her way through college, paying for anatomy class via a class anatomy.

Risky:

"Amid the welcoming fanfare of home-grown Texas pageantry, Spain's visiting monarch was gracious and regal despite 100-degree heat and a long flight as he stepped off the plane at Austin's plain little airport Friday."

From Christy Hoppe of *The Dallas Morning News*:
The reign of Spain stepped gamely from the plane.

Risky:

"Hundreds of people from squealing teen-agers to blue-haired matrons lined up at local post offices across America yesterday to buy the newly released Elvis Presley official U.S. postage stamp."

Taking risks: Why should you?

From Venita James of the *Arizona Republic:*
He ain't nuthin' but a postage stamp. But Elvis inspires the same cultish devotion on paper as in person.

Risky:
"Despite a rise in the numbers of people who have turned to vegetarianism in the United States in recent years and in spite of Americans' ever-growing concern with eating foods that are high in fat content, New Yorkers who eat out are eating more red meat."

From Rick Hampson of The Associated Press:
Sixty years after Prohibition ended and speakeasies closed, New Yorkers are again sneaking off to shadowy, masculine bastions to consume a forbidden substance. They're going to steakhouses to eat red meat.

Risky:
"One of the most fashionable new items in Virginia gun shops is the holster, say area gun shop owners. And those gun-owner utilities come in a wide array of exotic colors and fancy styles."

A fresh and no-risk approach from Earl Swift of the *Virginian-Pilot:*
How does an urban sophisticate stay cool when all around town, tempers are rising with the temperature?

Simple: The fashion-conscious carry their own heat — and they do it with an ever-widening choice of stylish holsters that dazzle the eye while pampering the python. From bright-colored, kicky little fanny packs to butter-soft leather shoulder rigs, holsters are flying off gun shop shelves and into the wardrobes of Virginians who want to look chic while never turning the other.

Taking risks: Why should you?

Risky:

"Bingo is enjoying a huge upswing in popularity in the area, say the game's many fans."

From Krys Stefansky of the *Virginian-Pilot*:

Couldn't have been worse timing.

Right in the middle of the U-Pick-M, a woman keels over and needs a doctor.

About 150 people, well, about 149 now, are dabbing the numbers they scribbled on their bingo cards and here's this distraction.

Aren't those who say *take a risk* really saying *be a writer? Don't* take risks — not with your copy, your audience, or your career. Instead, think hard and think for yourself. Know things. Make connections. Write smooth, energetic sentences. Put aside forever the trite, the threadbare, the formulaic. Use your imagination. In short, be at least as smart and entertaining a story-teller in print as you are in person. That's what *writers* do.

column

43

Missed opportunity

Creativity seeks stories, not reports

Many newspaper-of-record stories are routine and obvious, but they are must-do news assignments. They're sow's ear stories — vital to newspaper and reader but offering little that is fresh, unusual or even very complex. The challenge is to make them accurate, clear, conversational, brief and non-formulaic.

For sow's ear stories, that's challenge enough.

However, some stories offer another sort of challenge — and opportunity. We should approach those with minds wide open, with the creative person's natural inventiveness and curiosity. One of the chief tasks of a creative intellect is to see connections — to associate, analyze, extrapolate. Seeing only the obvious is a failure of both intellect and imagination, and in newspapers, it results in a failure to present the real story, the more interesting story, or the story within the story.

Consider the following, which appeared in a daily newspaper that serves a largely rural region. A high-powered Hollywood advertising agency had produced some television ads for Audi in one of the small communities served by the newspaper. The front-page story covering the event dealt only with the obvious: They came, they saw, they filmed. The lead has some writing problems, but its greater problem is missed opportunity. (The city and principals have new names. Otherwise, the lead is unchanged.)

> *'Buy an Audi,' Town Clerk Janie Smith quipped Wednesday when a 65-member Hollywood film crew finished its morning shoot of an Audi car commercial on Beauville's Main Street.*
> *Will wheat farmers start buying audis?*
> *Maybe not. But Beauville is apparently a good place to film a commercial.*
> *'They wanted an older farming community. They liked the looks of it,' Jon Noble, a town maintenance and utility worker, said about the Hollywood firm, Sanford Bowen Associates Inc., which shot the commercial for Audi.*

Starting a story with a quotation is always risky, but this one ("Buy an Audi") is especially weak. It's not much of a "quip," and it unleashes a non sequitur:

- An advertising agency is filming an Audi commercial in Beauville.
- Therefore, the Audi company wants wheat farmers to buy Audis.

Is the Audi company trying to get wheat farmers to buy Audis? Probably not: The car's niche market is the upscale boomer.

So what *is* going on? We don't know because the story doesn't tell us: What is the ad campaign's message, and why Beauville? The story deals only with the *what*, not the *why*. We read that the ads feature a father and daughter traveling in an Audi station wagon. That several other shiny new Audis are on hand, including a convertible. That a local man driving a tractor appears alongside the Audi in one segment. That the crew has cleared the scene of modern road signs and parked

'60s cars and pick-ups along Beauville's streets.

The only answer to *why* comes from a local utility worker, who says the ad folks "liked the looks of" Beauville. That's no answer. And no wonder — he's not the right one to ask. He has no facts, no solid information. Why not ask the agency reps or advertising crew? They could say something interesting even if only: "We wanted to play this upscale import against the backdrop of an older rural community." The *why* to that remark would yield even better material.

How do I know what agency or advertisers might say? I don't; I'm just guessing. And that's the problem: Stories that lack full information always make readers guess, and they shouldn't have to.

The advertising world has its reasons, and its reasons have to do with assumptions about its audience, about the culture, about psychology, about the image that manipulates. Treating this story as a small and obvious news item sacrificed a more interesting, substantive and enlightening story.

Even the best writers can leave holes in a story or fail to see the real story. To avoid those pitfalls, respect your own curiosity. Ask:

- Have I listened to my own questions?
- Have I asked those questions?
- Have I asked the right people?

The writer of the Audi story asked *why*, but he asked the wrong person. Getting something from the agency's crew shouldn't have been hard: The filming took two days. But if, for some reason, the reporter couldn't talk to the crew, that Hollywood agency has a phone number and every account has a manager.

Still, having said that, let's suppose we're line editors on deadline, and the story above is the story we get. It's too late to seize missed opportunity. There's no time to rewrite or to collect information not provided by the story. At that point, the best we can do, usually, is fix a story's mechanics. How could we quickly salvage this lead, both for form and content, and lose the non sequitur? Here's one way:

Will wheat country buy Audis?
Maybe not. But Audi advertisers have bought wheat country.

The best solution, though, would be to give the story back to the writer with a short list of salient questions. Give him another day. The story is not urgent; more critical is creating something interesting. By setting higher standards, you'll do the writer a favor as well as the reader.

44

Me, myself and I

Modesty covers a multitude of sins in first-person writing

Media writers are often advised to avoid first-person pronouns in their work, and for good reason. The greenest reporter knows there's no place for first-person pronouns in objective news coverage, and that focusing on oneself in analyses or opinion writing is suspect even if permissible. So this most obvious kind of writer intrusion is rarely a problem in "hard" news. It arises chiefly in columns, criticism and features.

The problem is one of focus. The best writers focus tightly and relentlessly upon some subject other than themselves. They are like cinematographers. They illumine the subject, and they themselves stay offstage. Sometimes they develop literary or rhetorical devices to help them stay out of the copy. Syndicated columnist Ellen Goodman, for example, often writes in the third person (*she*) when writing of herself. And Mike Royko, the late syndicated columnist, sometimes dispensed opinion through imagined conversations between created characters.

Such devices are alter egos that let the writer avoid that off-putting *me, myself* and *I*.

Unfortunately, as newspaper writers search for their own

strongest, most colorful and individual "voice," they sometimes latch onto an egocentric writing style that is as boorish as it is misguided. They've been admonished to tell stories, to "get the people in," to be human, personal and revealing. So they tell *their* stories, get *themselves* in, and the humanity they reveal is their own.

Do they never guess that most readers respond: *Who cares?*

The sad truth is that most people who cry *look at me* are not very interesting. And neither are writers who constantly write about themselves. It's true that some of the most memorable and affecting pieces we've read have been first-person accounts. But those were the exceptional accounts of exceptional events or people. Take Associated Press writer Tad Bartimus' prize-winning first-person story of her father's death. People die every day. But Ms. Bartimus' father died only once; it was an exceptional event matched by an exceptional treatment from a writer who did not ordinarily write about herself.

Effective first-person accounts in which the writer is the subject can teach us something about the human condition and the universality of human experience. They are both welcome and enriching. But when the subject is something or someone *other* than the writer and still the writer is in the story, the reader wants to say *you again?* In those cases, the writer is cheapened and the reader cheated.

Here are some examples.

■ A food writer's subject is the joy of canning. But she begins with a tedious and mawkish reminiscence on canning day at Auntie's farm.

■ A travel writer gives a detailed report on what he did in Belgium — rather than what the *reader* might similarly do.

■ A film critic doesn't review a newly released tearjerker so much as he reviews his own performance as a Sensitive Guy. He takes four paragraphs to say how hard the movie made him cry.

- A columnist on the work of a local artist: "I thought the small, dense works so different from the large airy ones greeting me in the foyer that I found it hard to believe they were from the same painter. When I mentioned it, he told me I was right — that he was in a sense different people when he created them."

How do we stay out and still stay personal? It's neither difficult nor a mystery. Reader-friendly writing focuses on the reader (and the subject) rather than on the writer:

- *Maybe you already know about the joys of canning. Maybe you've admired your own freshly filled Mason jars, immaculate and glowing on the shelf.*

- *If you find yourself in Brussels, consider renting a car for a side trip over the hump-backed bridges of Bruge.*

- *Just try to sit dry-eyed through 'Tijuana Tear-Jerker.'*

- *The small, dense canvases are so different from the large, open ones in the foyer that they seem the work of different painters. Yes, acknowledges the artist — in a sense, he was different people when he created them.*

Again, it's not that first-person pronouns are forbidden, or should be. If there's compelling and appropriate reason to use them, we needn't hesitate. Otherwise, we should be modest — and find interesting, imaginative and engaging ways to stay out of the work. After all, it's both better writing and better manners to aim our cameras at something other than ourselves.

column

45

Loaded language I

Avoiding the slant

Writers and editors spend a lot of time trying to find the right words. Should it be black or African-American? Native American or American Indian? Latino or Hispanic? Inuit or Alaskan or Eskimo?

And while we're busy with those right words, wrong words of other kinds creep in. The *style* of a word, even in the important issue of naming, is easy to spot and correct. But another kind of wrong word — the loaded word — demands more attention. Loaded language, potentially more hurtful for its subtlety, does real damage to fair and objective reporting.

Loaded language comes from reporter intrusion, whether witting or unwitting, and through two chief avenues.

■ Seeming or actual bias that creeps into news stories via slant or phrasing.

■ Problems with tone, taste, assumption or sensationalism.

No fair and reputable newspaper wants biased copy in its pages, and no fair reporter wants to write such copy. But the insidious thing about loaded language is that we often don't realize we're loading it. Writers tend to defend such phrasing by saying it's more interesting or colorful written that way, and to condemn critics as unimaginative and timid.

Choosing factual, objective language demands a keen conscience and mature self-awareness from the writer and a stern and critical vigilance from the editor. But it's worth it: Only neutral language can offer the readers an undistorted image of reality.

Take one metropolitan daily's story about the Supreme Court's 1992 decision to strike down the Minnesota ordinance outlawing cross-burnings, swastika displays or other acts of prejudice. Here's the story's lead. (The italics are mine.)

"The U.S. Supreme Court *dealt a blow* Monday to the national campaign to combat hate crimes, striking down as a violation of free speech a Minnesota city's ordinance that outlawed cross burnings.

"The ruling could *threaten* hate-crime statutes enacted in recent years by many other cities and 46 states. . . . Advocates, though, said they were *optimistic* that the laws would withstand legal challenges."

Our natural reaction to such language as "dealt a blow" or "threatened" is to suppose something bad happened. That terrible court decision just *dealt a blow* to those fighting *hate crimes*, of all things, and it's *threatening* such laudable efforts all over the country.

But couldn't we have said as well — in fact, *better* — that the court unanimously upheld constitutional rights to free speech? What did those justices really do? They struck down something they *unanimously*, conservative and liberal alike, judged a violation of First Amendment rights.

How would this story read it it were written in neutral, uncharged language? Here's such a lead, from the *Chicago Tribune*:

"A St. Paul ordinance that prohibits cross-burnings, Nazi swasti-

ka displays and other bias-motivated conduct violates the
Constitution's free-expression guarantees, the Supreme Court ruled
unanimously Monday."

"The ordinance discriminates on the basis of content by pun-
ishing only expressions of racial, gender or religious intolerance, said
Justice Antonin Scalia, who delivered the court's opinion. This kind
of selectivity, he declared, promotes unwarranted and illegal government censorship."

The following paragraph appeared in a major daily late in the
1992 presidential campaign. Here the language is more overtly
loaded, even opinionated.

"The *best news* for the two-party system, in the short term at
least, *might be a victory by Bill Clinton and the Democrats*, giving one
party control of both the White House and the Congress and an
opportunity to enact a leglislative program. By contrast, *a victory by
George Bush and the Republicans would lead to four more years of divided government by a minority lame-duck president, leading a party that
would be almost instantly obsessed with a struggle to choose his successor.*"

The writer takes it upon himself to state as fact two debatable
(not to mention *visionary*) opinions. He appears to be writing an
analysis, if not an editorial. But this passage appears in a news story
— where the reader has every right to expect objective and factual
reportage uncolored by reporter bias.

Here's a further example in which gratuitous reporter opinion
loads the language:

"Mr. Clinton and Mr. Yeltsin shared a pale yellow sofa in an
ornate sitting room at Blair House. . . . It was the first time the two

men met. But Mr. Yeltsin's initial remarks *could not have been what Mr. Clinton was seeking."*

Is the writer clairvoyant? How could that writer know not only what Clinton was *seeking*, but that this wasn't *it?*

Political stories, sensitive though they might be, are hardly the only hazards. Crime, police or trial stories often invite us to load or sensationalize our language or treatment. We'll discuss those stories in the next column.

46

Loaded language II

Readers have a right to fair and objective reporting

The last column discussed some hazards of loaded language. That's language that accompanies reporter intrusion — through seeming or actual bias or through problems with tone, taste, assumption or sensationalism.

Crime, police or trial stories often invite loaded language or sensationalism. In such stories, we sometimes find reporters (rather than some knowledgeable source) telling or interpreting — rather than *showing*. Someone in a tax evasion case has a "posh" suite in a "pricey" section of town. A man charged with child abuse wears a "sardonic smile" as he's escorted to the courtroom. A victim in a rape trial is referred to as "voluptuous." One reporter writes sneeringly of a defendant who shows up in court "carefully dressed in designer clothing" while another is equally scornful of one who looks "unkempt." In murder cases, we cast about for gimmicks or sexy details and in the process forget that someone died.

Loaded language is a habit of tabloid journalism, and it can be contagious.

Here, from the news columns of a large and respected newspaper, is one reporter's treatment of Woody Allen's courtroom appearance during his child sexual abuse case. (These are the *reporter's* words, not quotes from others.) "Mr. Allen sat on the stand with the hunched-over posture of someone who half-hoped to disappear by scrunching up into a small ball." The reporter went to to say that Allen looked "remarkably like a befuddled old man." That he "sounded like a bright but poorly prepared graduate student struggling with a crucial oral examination." That "the trial was a highly unwelcome surrender of artistic control over the Allen persona."

The reporter also characterized Eleanor Alter, the lawyer questioning Allen, as one who "nagged and hectored," as "a dogged but often incomprehensible questioner who seems to have trouble constructing any sentence more complicated than subject-verb-object." He described Elkan Abramowitz, Woody Allen's lawyer, as a man with "an odd gait that suggests his shoes may be too tight."

In short, the readers got more reporter than reporting in that story.

Lampooning is easy, and public figures have little defense against it. Lampooning can be interesting and even fun in certain kinds of stories. But in serious journalism, it isn't fair, objective or responsible.

Below are two examples of vigilant editing from a major metropolitan daily — as they were submitted to the editors, and as they were published.

Original: "A former Dallas nightclub owner won't spend a single day in prison for killing his girlfriend last October.

"John Joseph Caulfield, former owner of Stan's Blue Note on Greenville Avenue, received 10 years probation and a $10,000 fine Friday for the Oct. 30 death of Kendall Dodson."

Edited: "A former Dallas nightclub owner will not go to prison for killing his girlfriend in October.

"John Joseph Caulfield, former owner of Stan's Blue Note on Greenville Avenue, received 10 years probation and a $10,000 fine Friday for the Oct. 30 death of Kendall Dodson."

The language in the original is loaded because there's only one way we can read that a killer "won't spend a single day in prison" — and that's with a *tsk, tsk*. The original tells us this is bad. The edited version plays it straight and lets the readers decide.

Here's the second example.

Original: "A Dallas County jury decided Thursday that John Joseph Caulfield loved his girlfriend to death."

"After deliberating almost two hours, the nine women and three men jurors convicted Mr. Caulfield of the Oct. 30 murder. They concluded that a drunken, jealous anger drove the former owner of Stan's Blue Note to fatally shoot 27-year-old Kendall Dodson."

Edited: "Former Dallas nightclub owner John Joseph Caulfield was convicted Thursday of murdering his girlfriend in what prosecutors called a drunken rage."

"A Dallas County jury of nine women and three men convicted Mr. Caulfield after deliberating almost two hours."

"Prosecutors had argued that jealousy drove the former owner of Stan's Blue Note to fatally shoot 27-year-old Kendall Dodson."

The words "loved his girlfriend to death" probably seemed a good idea at the time. But they risk seeming flippant if not callous. Anyone whose life has been touched by murder knows that murder is not really Damon Runyon or True Detective territory. A woman is dead, and she wasn't loved to death. The edited version is mindful of that fact.

Loaded language II

And in terms of simple accuracy, we must also observe that the jury did not decide that Caulfield "loved his girlfriend to death." The *reporter* decided that, apparently. The jury decided only that he killed her.

Journalists have feelings and opinions, of course, but objective writers and editors try not to load those feelings and opinions onto the back of the language. Readers have a right to their opinions, too — without their understanding first being filtered through the screen of someone's else's perception.

column

47

Pretty lies

Precision and accuracy strip away
the mask of euphemism

A bank I patronize has this sign in its drive-in window: "For your convenience, have your transaction ready." Now, having the transaction ready has nothing to do with customer convenience; it has to do with efficiency and courtesy to others. And how much more effective that truth would be than the meaningless euphemism *for your convenience.*

Another bank has this sign: "For your convenience, all transactions enacted after 3 p.m. will be recorded the following business day." Here, the euphemism helps an inconvenience masquerade as a convenience.

A department store set up a "courtesy desk" for the "convenience" of its shoppers during a recent Christmas season. Customers were obliged to check their packages at the desk: They must stop, stand in line, unload and get a receipt before they were free to shop. And they had to repeat the procedure upon leaving the store. In the meantime, someone else had what belonged to them, and they had no access to their purchases.

That's a *convenience?*

In clear and accurate communication, euphemisms are not the

way to treat people. There are ways to communicate that are both inoffensive *and* accurate, and good communicators will find those ways. The first bank's sign, for example, could read: "Avoid delays by having your transaction ready" or "As a courtesy to others, please have your transaction ready." Both are accurate statements and also would be more effective in eliciting the desired behavior. The second sign could drop the reference to convenience; customers understand reality. And the department store could stop calling its parcel check-in system a "convenience" and say honestly that it is a device to control shoplifting. There's nothing wrong with that, and most people would be glad to cooperate if it meant curbing theft. Business seldom does what it does for the customers' convenience. We know that. And we'd respect the business world more if it would just tell the truth.

If euphemisms abound in business, they seem almost mandatory in government. A Cold War joke goes this way:

During an important meeting between Western and Eastern powers, the Soviet and American leaders challenged each other to a foot race. The U.S. leader won, and the American press reported: "The president defeated the chairman of the USSR in a two-man foot race yesterday."

Now, the Soviet leader's defeat posed a problem for the Soviet press, which was charged with presenting things in a positive light or as a victory for Communism. But the undaunted Soviets reported: "The USSR's chairman and the U.S. president participated in a foot race in Moscow yesterday. Our leader brought honor to the Soviet Union by finishing second. The president of the United States, however, finished next to last."

The Cold War is over, but that's still a good story because it illustrates how euphemisms can shape perceptions.

The euphemism is an expression chosen for its ability to lay a smooth patina over a rough truth. Thus, we call the toilet a *powder room*. When people die, we say they *pass away*. We still term chicken *dark* or *white* meat because of the Victorians' reluctance to say breast or thigh.

So what's wrong with that? Sounds like the euphemism could oil the rough waters of otherwise blunt discourse. And it does. It allows us the social grace of the little white lie, which harms no one.

Which harms no one. Those are the crucial words. Social euphemisms merely prettify, but others can distort and deceive. The dangerous euphemism is that born in the public arena — in political, military and commercial sectors.

Governments excel in euphemism for obvious reasons. The intolerable somehow has to be made to seem tolerable — and the technique for accomplishing that illusion is through a welter of either positive or bewildering words.

During the Vietnam era, the United States bombed Hanoi and called the action a "protective reaction air strike." During the Reagan administration, the MX missile was the "peacekeeper." American policy in Lebanon in the early '80s was termed "aggressive self-defense." The U.S. attack on Granada was billed a "pre-dawn military insertion." Pentagon brass has termed military disasters "near-triumphs." Killing civilians during the Gulf War was "collateral damage." Great Britain called the sinking of the Belgrano during the Falklands war a "media embarrassment."

Such euphemisms and gobbledygook abound from the highest to the lowest levels of bureaucracy. A Texas prison warden said in a radio interview that the job of the prison was not to punish the inmates, but to "create functioning social units."

The mask of the euphemism is worn everywhere. We don't kill people; *we take them out.* Terrorists don't murder; they *execute.* Stalin *liquidated.* Hitler had a *final solution.* Death camps were *work* camps. Famine is *food shortage*; starvation becomes *mortality from disease due to malnutrition*. Advertisers peddle a medicine for *motion discomfort*, rather than for sea- or air-sickness. "Campaign rhetoric" means the lies we *expect* to hear.

Words matter; they bear the weight of both the truth and the lie. While a pretty lie is easier to listen to than an ugly truth, it is truth that has force and impact, and it is truth that the public really needs. Journalists should not traffic in euphemisms — they, too, can be seduced by pretty lies, but their charge is to find and deliver the truth.

Sexism in print

The excesses of political correctness have hushed legitimate complaint

Many who comment on the language have been relatively silent of late on sexist, racist or ageist language. The excesses of political correctness have hushed them. An atmosphere of stridence, silliness, hostility and imagined grievance leave little room for people who wish to be sensible and constructive.

A major problem with the excesses of political correctness is that those excesses help scotch legitimate observations concerning "isms," whether of sex, race, or age. Case in point: This column is years old and not once has it addressed sexism in print. That's not because such problems don't exist, but because I'm loath to be numbered among those who charge (for example) that "manhole" is sexist.

Nonsense and backlash aside, sexism in print still presents a problem for fair, accurate communication. True, the examples are neither as blatant nor as pervasive as they once were. But it's probably equally true that any "ism" is more pernicious for subtlety. It's easier to eradicate the broad or crude lampoon than the subtle expression tied to cultural conditioning.

Here's how four sexist assumptions still manifest themselves in media writing:

- *The death penalty will be sought against a man who pleaded guilty to raping and murdering a doctor's wife last year.* (Television newscast)
- *An Illinois man and his wife were charged here Tuesday with illegal possession and intent to sell hashish worth about $5,000.* (Newspaper story)
- *Woman photographer wins sabbatical.* (Headline)
- *At 36, she's still a knockout, her clear English skin and sparkling blue eyes set off by auburn curls.* (Column about a woman who had won a local political office)

Each of those common and seemingly benign passages shows sexism. We can be sure of that because each shows a treatment of a woman that we would not accord to a man. Knowing this, we can discover what the assumption behind the treatment is.

The first passage reveals the assumption that a woman is defined by her relationship to a man. Here, her identity is that she's a *doctor's wife*. Imagine this: *The death penalty will be sought against a man who pleaded guilty to murdering a doctor's husband last year.* That word *husband* is so odd that the passage at first bewilders us. Upon reflection, we realize that we would identify a male victim as a man or by his profession, but not by his marital status.

The second passage is similar, with a twist. That we write *a man and his wife* suggests ownership — we don't write *a husband and wife* or *a man and a woman*. It also suggests that a man always remains a man, but at marriage a woman becomes a *wife*.

When Wendy Gramm, who is married to Texas Senator Phil Gramm, became chair of the Commodities Futures Trading Commission, a Texas newspaper ran this headline: "Gramm's wife to head U.S. panel." Wendy Gramm already had a secure public identity, especially in Texas — she'd been the director of the Office of Information and Regulatory Affairs at the Office of Management and Budget. Yet the headline writer must have thought Wendy Gramm's position as a wife would identify her better than even her own name.

The third example shows the decrepit stereotype that professionals are male unless otherwise identified. We see a similar assumption in racism — that everyone is white unless otherwise identified. Consider that "black poet Rita Dove" is almost a boiler-plate label for this former poet laureate.

The final example shows both sexism and ageism. The assumption here is in part that a woman's appearance merits comment, whether she defies or exemplifies a stereotype, whether her appearance has anything to do with the story, or whether we would comment on a man's appearance in the same context. One can't imagine, in an election story, such simpering remarks as those above about a *man's* skin, eyes and hair.

The second problem in the final example is the assumption that a woman is over the hill while still young: "At 36, she's *still* a knockout." Why the *still?* Robert Redford and Clint Eastwood played romantic leads at 60; when they were 36, did anyone say they were *still* hunks? It's no more absurd applied to them than it is applied to women.

Men by no means escape the problem of sexism in print, however. But — since one of the stereotypes of men is that they're the perpetrators of sexism — they have few protectors against its damages. Here are two passages from two newspapers:

- *They write to ask if their husbands have lovers, or whether their relatives are trying to cheat them out of money.*
- *She has been called 'the Dear Abby' of the food section. But this columnist deals in broken diets, not broken hearts, and in runaway cholesterol counts, not runaway husbands.*

Sexism in print

Only men cheat? Only men abandon their families? *Husbands* in both examples should have been *spouses* or *mates*.

These kinds of problems are hard to stamp out because they're common and relatively subtle. And they often go unchallenged — sometimes, admittedly, because we're sick on an overdose of foolishness masquerading as political correctness. But that shouldn't quiet legitimate complaint.

49

Politispeak

Pols often disfigure figures of speech

Most political scandals spin off a few delightful snickers in the form of the principals' verbal gaffes and lapses. Even grim Watergate gave us a world-class euphemism for *lying*: "That statement is inoperable."

But Washington, D.C., hasn't been a lot of laughs lately. The acidic political atmosphere makes one long for the good old days when politicians said the darnedest things. When George Bush was once in hot water, for example, he explained: "We have had triumphs, we have made mistakes, we have had sex."

What he meant to say was: "We have had had *setbacks*."

The former president also gave us a chuckle when he quoted some lyrics from the Nitty Gritty Dirt Band and attributed them to the "Nitty Ditty Nitty Gritty Great Bird."

Remember Mr. Bush's attachment to the word *thing*? It started with the *vision thing* and progressed to the *post-Vietnam thing*, the *gender thing* and the *hostage thing*. He referred to vomiting at a banquet in Japan as the *stomach thing*. He called plans to do a film about his family's Maine vacations the *roots thing*. He asked space shuttle astronauts about the *deployment thing*. And at a New Jersey rehabilitation center, he asked about the *withdrawal thing*.

But if George Bush was amusing talking to the folks at the rehab center, Sen. Ted Kennedy was hilarious chatting up a patron at the soup kitchen. "Do you come here often?" he asked.

Former president Gerald Ford tickled us with unintentional word play, too. "If President Lincoln were alive today," he said, "he'd roll over in his grave."

Most politicians quickly learn the hazards of dealing in a foreign tongue. Ronald Reagan once declared that there was no word for *freedom* in the Russian language. His statement lost its drama when those who knew promptly pointed out that the Russian word for freedom was *svoboda*.

And John F. Kennedy, urbane as he seemed when he told the roaring Berlin crowds "Ich bin ein Berliner," also unwittingly created a linguistic gaffe. In Germany, a "berliner" is also a pastry. And those who speak German assure me that one does not properly precede a nationality with the article *a, an* or *the*. Or, in this case, *ein*. The nationality stands alone: *Ich bin Berliner*. So some of that German audience's roar of delight at JFK's words was not because he said "I am a Berliner," but because he said, "I am a jelly doughnut."

Metaphor can also get politicians in trouble. Take this one from Jesse Jackson: "If we crush the grapes of hope into raisins of despair, they may not be able to bounce back in the fall."

Florid oratory is one thing; plain old bafflegab is another. A member of the Baltimore City Council once described an issue as "a little snowball that rolled down the hill, that gathered moss and, when it got to the bottom, became a big mushroom."

Ponder that.

Canadian politician Robert Thompson also attempted a snowball metaphor: "If this thing starts to snowball, it will catch fire right across the country."

In 1980, Sen. Howard Cannon lost track of body parts when

he said: "The advent of these sleek coaches should provide a shot in the arm to both legs of Nevada's passenger train system."

Former Chicago mayor Jane Byrne's tongue twisted her vocabulary when she blended *fruitful* and *worthy* and got *fruitworthy*.

Another former Chicago mayor, Richard Daley (the first one), was famous for his linguistic creations. He once promised, for example, greater and greater *platitudes* of achievements. Often, Daley's gobbledygook made a weird sort of sense—as when he said: "I resent your *insinuendos*." During the 1968 Democratic Convention riots, Daley assured: "The policeman isn't there to *create* disorder. He's there to *preserve* disorder."

Those disfigured figures of speech come from contemporary "mixaphorians." But the skill existed well before the sound bite came along to record it. Sir Boyle Roche, an 18th century Irish parliamentarian, constructed this memorable statement: "Mr. Speaker, I smell a rat. I see him forming in the air and darkening the sky. But I'll nip him in the bud."

Maybe that's what we need from Washington rhetoric these days — less meanness, more metaphor.

column

50

Tips for coaching writers

Creating the right climate promotes teamwork

Editors who work directly with writers often seek ways of making
their editing sessions with writers more productive, constructive and
amiable. They know their one-on-one sessions are critical and can
either preserve or destroy a healthy working relationship with the
writer. So they must constantly balance the nurturing that builds
trust with a candor that could destroy it.

It's all too true that some writers say they want criticism until
they get it. But the best writers make the editor's job easier: They
seek constructive criticism, appreciate it, and know how to use it to
their benefit.

Below are some tips for creating a climate for healthy
writer/editor negotiations.

■ Begin with a sincere and *specific* review of what the writers
  do well — not as a sop, but to help them recognize and
  build on their strengths. Use examples: Some writers do
  not know what they do well and have to be shown.

■ Ask writers if they are satisfied with their story or approach
  before advancing your own opinion. The answers can be

revealing. They often already know that a story is flawed; sometimes they even know why. Constructive teamwork is easier and more productive if you create an environment in which writers are their own critics. When they, rather than you, set forth flaws, you can become partners in the effort to improve.

■ Launch into the critical portion of the session quickly and courageously, with candor and directness. Maintain eye contact and speak gently and in good will. Remember that some writers are notoriously sensitive, but don't pull punches; even sensitive writers hope for a fair but no-nonsense assessment of their work. Don't insult, on the other hand, and don't confuse bluntness or rudeness with candor. Constantly gauge the writer's reaction to your words to avoid plunging heedlessly past a rough moment. Acknowledge and discuss such moments so they don't sour the whole session.

■ Treat writers as equals — don't operate from a position of authority. You might advance the notion, for example, that you speak as an intelligent reader rather than as an expert or critic. The orientation of intelligent reader gives you carte blanche: You cannot be wrong about your responses. And writers will welcome an intelligent reader's honest response to their work.

■ Be concrete. Keep focused on the writer's work. Don't generalize or wander. Support your words with mark-ups of the writers' works, and give them a copy of the marked work so they can consider it later at leisure and in a relaxed setting.

Tips for coaching writers

■ Feel free to use humor if that's your style, but don't say anything that can be construed as making fun. Gentle humor helps people relax, makes the session fun, and softens criticism without compromising it.

■ Express the highest standards. Empathetically acknowledge such newsroom realities as deadline pressures, heavy work loads, sources who don't call back, etc., but emphasize that professionals aim for excellence despite those realities. (Sometimes problems are offered as defenses, but problems are reasons, not excuses.) Respond with something like *sure, that challenge will always be with us*, and move on.

■ Writers (not you) should cut and rewrite. When you habitually do the laborious but crucial rewriting, you get better and better at it, but the writer does not. A writer's main responsibility is to become his or her own best editor — try not to get in the way of that responsibility.

■ Criticize the product, not the person. Not: *Your leads are dull*, but: *These two stories have dull tops. How could we brighten them?* Not: *Your grammar is poor*, but: *The grammatical errors in this story get in the way of its message.*

■ Don't overwhelm writers with too much to fix. Concentrate on several important aspects of writing whose improvement would make the work better overnight. Solve problems one at a time. Writers with big problems need to get some successes under their belts. Help them do that.

Tips for coaching writers

- When discussing writing, don't confuse evaluating and teaching. Just telling somebody that something is wrong is not teaching. Develop a lexicon for discussing the subtleties of writing and be prepared to communicate that information clearly, to show examples of exactly what you mean. Avoid saying *it just sounds better* or *I can't explain it, but.* . . . Those words frustrate people who want specific and clear direction.

- If there are serious problems, make it clear that you expect those to go away within a specified period, but couch that goal from the writer's point of view. For example, instead of saying I (or *we*) want, wish, need, say: *You'll* want to improve in this area; *you'll* be pleased with your progress when; *you'll* be more satisfied with your performance if; *you'll* feel better about yourself when you get this straightened out. . . .

- Finally, *listen.* The best editors put their egos aside and try to learn from the session, too.

Obviously, the responsibility for making the writer-editor relationship work is not entirely the editor's. Like any good relationship, both parties have to work at it. So we could devise a similar tip sheet for writers. But that's a subject for another column.

Index